Date

BOOKS BY P. G. WODEHOUSE

❧

Service with a Smile
The Ice in the Bedroom
How Right You Are, Jeeves
French Leave
A Few Quick Ones
Cocktail Time
The Butler Did It
America, I Like You
Bertie Wooster Sees It Through
The Return of Jeeves
Pigs Have Wings
Angel Cake
The Old Reliable
Nothing Serious
The Mating Season
Uncle Dynamite
Spring Fever
Full Moon
Joy in the Morning
Money in the Bank
Quick Service
Eggs, Beans and Crumpets
Uncle Fred in the Springtime
The Code of the Woosters
Summer Moonshine
The Crime Wave at Blandings
Laughing Gas
Young Men in Spats
The Luck of the Bodkins
Blandings Castle
Brinkley Manor
Thank You, Jeeves
Heavy Weather
Mulliner Nights
Hot Water
If I Were You!

Big Money
Very Good, Jeeves
Summer Lightning
Mr. Mulliner Speaking
Money for Nothing
Meet Mr. Mulliner
Bill the Conqueror
Sam in the Suburbs
The Small Bachelor
Carry On, Jeeves
Divots
He Rather Enjoyed It
Leave It to Psmith
Jeeves
White Hope
Golf without Tears
Mostly Sally
Three Men and a Maid
The Little Warrior
Indiscretions of Archie
Love among the Chickens
The Intrusions of Jimmy
The Prince and Betty
Something New
Uneasy Money
The Little Nugget
A Gentleman of Leisure
A Damsel in Distress
Piccadilly Jim

COLLECTIONS

The Most of P. G. Wodehouse
Wodehouse on Golf
The Weekend Wodehouse
Nothing but Wodehouse

AUTHOR! AUTHOR!

P. G. Wodehouse

New York   *1962*
SIMON AND SCHUSTER

LIBRARY OF CONGRESS CATALOG CARD NUMBER: 62–12415
MANUFACTURED IN THE UNITED STATES OF AMERICA
BY H. WOLFF BOOK MFG. CO., INC., NEW YORK

To
Peter Schwed
But for whom . . .

Introduction

It was only a few months ago, though I had been receiving them for more than fifty years, that the thought occurred to me that an instructive book could be made of these letters written to me by Pelham Grenville ("Plum") Wodehouse, eliminating the purely private passages which would be unintelligible to anyone but myself.

When I say instructive, I mean instructive to young authors, for they are full of sound advice on the writing of fiction; and to the beginner, who is learning his trade by the laborious process of trial and error, advice from a craftsman of Plum's caliber should be of considerable value.

In my impecunious youth in San Francisco, an equally impecunious friend from Omaha, with whom I had worked for a pittance on a ranch in Mendocino County, near Russian River, walked with me one day on Market Street and revealed a scheme whereby we could both make a vast fortune. His idea was that we should combine what small amount of cash we had and insert advertisements in the San Francisco papers stating that we were prepared to criticize and revise short stories and novels at a fee of so much per thousand words, and for a further fee would advise the writers of these how best to earn a living from authorship. He said, with some accuracy, that most people in San Francisco were writing or planning to write, so why should we not make a quick buck by telling them how to do it.

I was horrified and firmly refused, much to his regret, but without impairing our friendship. I said I knew nothing about writing fiction, and he said he knew rather less than I did but seemed puzzled that I should feel that that mattered.

Now, Plum, I think, would have been qualified even then to take on such a project. Almost from the very beginning he knew his job. As Peter Quennell wrote of him not long ago, "Though not one non-literary reader in a thousand will lift his eyes from the page to consider Wodehouse as an artist, a fellow-hack cannot *fail to admire the extraordinary skill with which . . . he goes about his business. Every sentence has a job to do and—in spite of the air of lunatic irresponsibility which hangs around a Wodehouse novel—does it neatly and efficiently. Bertie Wooster may live in a perpetual haze, but P. G. Wodehouse knows at any moment of the story exactly what he is aiming for."*

Plum and I were boys together sixty-odd years ago at the school founded by Shakespeare's friend Edward Alleyn at Dulwich just outside London—the "Valley Fields" of his books, Sam in the Suburbs, Big Money, The Butler Did It *and* The Ice in the Bed-room*—and when he left at the. age of eighteen he became a clerk in the Hong Kong and Shanghai Bank in Lombard Street.*

He was in the bank two years, and during that time, working at night, he wrote stories, articles, and verses with great assiduity but with very little. success. However, if a writer keeps on writing, something generally breaks eventually. There was an evening pa-per in those days called the Globe, *which carried on its front pages a humorous column entitled "By the Way," and Plum had from time to time contributed unpaid paragraphs and verses to it in the hope of catching the editor's eye. In September 1902, to his pro-found astonishment, he was offered the. job of conducting this column. As the salary was the stupendous one of three pounds (fifteen dollars) a week, a sum on which one could live with com-fort in those golden days, he felt that the time had come to resign from the bank and turn pro.*

It proved to be a wise move. His work at the Globe *was over by noon, and he had all the rest of his time for free-lancing. And while conditions at the turn of the. century were not too good for writers at the top of the tree, the big prices being still in the dis-tant future, they were excellent for an industrious young fellow who asked no more than to pick up the occasional half guinea. There were so many morning papers and evening papers and weekly papers that he was practically sure of selling his stuff somewhere if the stamps and envelopes held out. Plum began to get what he calls "audience response." from the men in the editorial chairs. His contributions appeared fairly regularly in* Punch, *and once or twice he even got a short story into the* Strand *Magazine,*

8

which for a young writer in England in those days was roughly equivalent to being awarded the Order of the Garter. His savings mounted up, and in the spring of 1904 he found himself sufficiently opulent to do what he had always dreamed of doing—pay a visit to America.

It had to be a brief visit, for the Globe's limit for staff vacations was five weeks, and in 1904 it took eight days to cross the Atlantic, but he was in New York for two and a half weeks and enjoyed every minute of it. And on his return to London he found that it had done him good professionally. It is hard to realize now, when after breakfasting at the Berkeley the traveler crosses the ocean and dines the same night at the Stork Club, but in 1904 anyone in the London writing world who had been to America was regarded with awe and looked upon as an authority on that terra incognita. As Plum put it in a semiautobiographical book which he wrote some years ago:

"After that trip to New York I was someone who counted. The manner of editors changed towards me. Where before it had been 'Throw this man out,' they now said 'Come in, my dear fellow, come in and tell us all about America.' When some intricate aspect of American politics had to be explained to the British public, it was 'Ask Wodehouse. Wodehouse will know.' My income rose like a rocketing pheasant. I made £505.1.7 in 1906 and £527.17.1 in 1907 and was living, I suppose, on about £203.4.9. In fact, if on November 17, 1907, I had not bought a secondhand Darracq car for £450 (and smashed it up in the first week) I should soon have been one of those economic royalists who get themselves so disliked. This unfortunate venture brought my capital back to where it had started, and a long and dusty road had to be travelled before my finances were in a state sufficiently sound to justify another visit to the land of my dreams.

"I have often wondered why all my life I have looked on America in that light. I had no affiliations with the country. My father had spent most of his life in Hong Kong. So had two of my uncles. My eldest brother was out there. You would have expected that it would have been the Orient that called to me. 'Pu₁ me somewheres east of Suez' you would have pictured me saying

to myself. But it hadn't worked out that way. People would see me walking along with a glassy look in my eyes and my mouth hanging open as if I had adenoids and would whisper to each other 'He's thinking of America.' And they were right."

It was in 1909 that he was able to cross the Atlantic again. The boats were quicker now, but even so he expected to remain only three weeks in New York. But just as he was preparing to pack and return to the salt mines a strange thing happened. He had brought with him a couple of short stories, and he sold one of them to the Cosmopolitan *and the other to* Collier's, *for $200 and $300 respectively, both on the same morning. That was in those days roughly equivalent to £40 and £60, and to one whose highest prices for similar efforts had been at the most £10, the discovery that American editors were prepared to pay on such a scale was like finding a rich and affectionate uncle from Australia. This, he felt, was the place for him. He realized, of course, that New York was more expensive than London, but even so one could surely live there practically forever on $500, especially as there were always the* Cosmopolitan *and* Collier's *standing by with their cornucopias, all ready to start pouring.*

To seize pen and paper and mail his resignation to the Globe *was the work of an instant. He took a room at a hotel in Greenwich Village and settled in with a secondhand typewriter and plenty of paper, prepared to fight it out on these lines if it took all summer.*

At the time when the first of these letters reached me, I, too, after some unprofitable years passed in picking lemons on a ranch in Southern California, prospecting in the Mojave Desert, and making a number of voyages on a number of tramp ships, had become a writer, mostly of sea stories, and was selling some of them to magazines in England and to the pulps in America, my chief means of support being Adventure, *then edited by Arthur Sullivant Hoffman.*

I begin these letters with one written soon after I was demobilized from the Army. Plum had been rejected for military service because of bad eyesight. I had not heard from him during the war.

W. TOWNEND

1920–1940

Arrandale Avenue
Great Neck
Long Island, N.Y.
February 28, 1920

Dear Bill,

Your letter arrived this morning, forwarded on from the *Saturday Evening Post*, and it's great to know that you're all right and selling stories all over the place. I've seen several of them in *Adventure*. I particularly liked "In the Stokehold."

Since we last corresponded, all sorts of things have been happening to me. At the beginning of the war I struck a bad patch and had grave doubts as to whether I would be able to keep the wolf the right side of the door. I had a certain facility for dialogue and a nice light comedy touch—at least, I thought it nice—but I couldn't sell a story anywhere. If you remember, I started off with a rush in 1909 by selling a couple to the *Cosmopolitan* and *Collier's*, but both magazines lost their grip after that and never came through again, and about the time of my marriage—September 30, 1914—the pulps, on which I was relying for the three square meals a day, also let me down. If it hadn't been for Frank Crowninshield, the editor of *Vanity Fair*, liking my stuff and taking all I could do—articles, not fiction—I should have been very much up against it.

Vanity Fair is a swanky magazine "devoted to Society and the Arts," and I used to write about half of it each month under a number of names—P. G. Wodehouse, Pelham Grenville, J. Plum, C. P. West, P. Brooke-Haven, and J. Walker Williams were some of them. The payment wasn't high, but high enough to keep me going, and if ever I needed a financial shot in the arm, it was then.

When Ethel and I got married, she had seventy-five dollars and I had fifty, and I remember the pang of envy I felt when we fetched up at The Little Church Around the Corner and the clergyman who was going to marry us bounded in and told us he had just made ten thousand bucks on the Stock Exchange. All through the ceremony I could see his eyes sparkling as he thought of it. I had the feeling that his mind wasn't really on his job, but he fixed us up all right, and we took the train to Bellport, Long Island, where we had rented a moth-eaten old shack for twenty-five dollars the first month and twenty after that. The home comforts were fairly slim, but I found it a great place to work and in the intervals of writing articles for *Vanity Fair* was able to finish a novel called *Something New*, which I hoped I might be able to sell to *Mumsey's* or one of the other pulps.

But I wasn't feeling too good. *Vanity Fair* had only just started, and these new magazines have a nasty way of folding after the seventh issue. If it did suddenly call it a day, I asked myself, Where would I get off? It was a pretty testing period and affected my nervous system quite a good deal, inclining me to jump at sudden noises and to think that I was being followed about by little men with black beards.

I was plugging along like this, the wolf still outside the door but sticking around and licking its lips in a meaning manner, when suddenly everything changed. The sun shone out, the United States Marines arrived, and the millennium set in. The *Saturday Evening Post* bought *Something New*, a miracle which absolutely stunned me, as I had never even considered the possibility of a long story by an unknown author having a chance there. Since then I have had three more serials in the *S.E.P.*—*Uneasy Money*, *Piccadilly Jim*, and *A Damsel in Distress*. They gave me a raise with each one—$3,500, $5,000, $7,500, and for the *Damsel* $10,000—so that now I can afford an occasional meat meal, not only for self but for wife and resident kitten and bulldog, all of whom can do with a cut off the joint.

But my big source of income these last years has been from the theater. I teamed up with Guy Bolton and Jerome Kern and we started doing musicals together. We wrote a fairly successful show called *Have a Heart* and then had a terrific smash with a thing called *Oh Boy*, after which all the managers were after us with commissions. One season Guy and I actually had five shows running simultaneously on Broadway, and about a dozen companies out on the road.

Guy and I clicked from the start like a couple of sailors on shore leave. He is one of the best fellows I ever met and the supreme worker of all time. I help him as much as I can with the "book" end of the things, but he really does the whole job and I just do the lyrics, a simple and pleasant task when one has Jerry to work with. Jerry generally does the melody first and I put words to it. W. S. ("Savoy Operas") Gilbert always said that a lyrist can't do decent stuff that way, but I don't agree with him, not as far as I'm concerned, anyway. If I write a lyric without having to fit it to a tune, I always make it too much like a set of light verse, much too regular in meter. I think you get the best results by giving the composer his head and having the lyrist follow him. For instance, the refrain of one of the songs in *Oh Boy* began "If every day you bring her diamonds and pearls on a string." I couldn't have thought of that, if I had done the lyric first, in a million years. Why, dash it, it doesn't *scan*. But Jerry's melody started off with a lot of twiddly little notes, the first thing emphasized being the "di" of "diamonds," and I just tagged along after him. Another thing . . . all this must be boring you stiff, but I thought I'd mention it . . . is that when you have the melody, you can see which are the musical high spots in it and can fit the high spots of the lyric to them. Anyway, that's how I like working, and to hell with any- one who says I oughtn't to.

In spite of all this theater activity, I have managed to write one or two short stories for the *S.E.P.* and I am now doing a serial for *Collier's* and another for—if you'll believe it—the *Woman's Home Companion*. Heaven knows what a woman's magazine wants with my sort of stuff, but they are giving me fifteen thou- sand of the best for it.

⌖

The *Collier's* serial was *The Little Warrior*, the *Woman's Home Com- panion's* a story which was published in book form in America as *Three Men and a Maid* and in England as *The Girl on the Boat*. The short stories which I mention were the first of the Jeeves stories, and by Jeeves stories I mean Jeeves stories in the deepest and fullest sense.

Actually, Jeeves made his first appearance in a morceau called *Extricating Young Gussie*, but if ever there was a bit part, his was it. He had two lines. One was "Mrs. Gregson to see you, sir," the other "Very good, sir. Which suit will you wear?"

At this point—early 1916—Bertie Wooster hogged the entire show and I never looked on Jeeves as anything but just one of the extras, a nonentity who might consider himself lucky if he got even two lines. It was only when I was writing a thing called *The Artistic Career of Corky*—late 1916—that he respectfully elbowed Bertie to one side and took charge.

Nobody has ever called Bertram Wooster one of our brightest minds, his friend Corky had possibly even less of what it takes to solve life's difficulties, and they were faced by a major problem. Being a conscientious artist, I simply could not let either of them suddenly have a brilliant idea for solving and yet somebody had to have one or the story could not be written. In the upshot, the chap who had the brilliant idea was me. Why not groom this bit player Jeeves for stardom? I said to myself. Why not, I said, still soliloquizing, make him a bird with a terrific brain who comes to Bertie's rescue whenever the latter gets into a jam? "Eureka!" I would have cried, only I didn't want to steal Archimedes' stuff, and I got down to it without delay.

"Jeeves," says Bertie on page four of *The Artistic Career of Corky*, "we want your advice. And from now on," he might have added, "you get equal billing."

P.G.W.

Arrandale Avenue
Great Neck
March 23, 1920

Dear Bill,

You *would* ask me if those five shows I said Guy Bolton and I had on B'way simultaneously were all successes. No, laddie, they were not, but far otherwise. One—*The Riviera Girl*—was sort of semi, two—*Leave It to Jane* and *Oh Boy* (carrying on strongly from 1916)—were big hits, and the other two—*The Rose of China* and a revue called *Miss 1917*—were about the most colossal flops in the history of the stage, and we are trying to forget them. They were disasters, and nobody to blame but us, for we were given excellent casts and lavish productions, particularly for the revue, which was put on by Flo Ziegfeld and Charlie Dillingham. Flo contributed all the girls from the Ziegfeld *Follies* and the music was by Jerry Kern and Victor Herbert, but we closed after thirty-six performances. All I got out of it was a bull-dog, given to me by Zitelka Dolores, one of the cast. He is a noble animal and the light of the home. Name Sammy.

The whole trouble was that we took on much too much work and did it much too quickly. You can't write three big musical shows at the same time and hope to do anything good. The next two we did—*Oh, Lady! Lady!* at the Princess, following *Oh Boy*, which moved to another theater, and *The Girl Behind the Gun*—we took our time, and they were both smash hits. You may have seen the latter. It's playing at the Winter Garden in London with George Grossmith and Leslie Henson. English title, *Kissing-Time*. I believe Henson is wonderful in it.

Here are the answers to your questions:

(1) Usually I'm pretty slow, but lately I have been writing stories at terrific speed. I've started a habit of rushing through them and then working over them very carefully, instead of try-ing to get the first draft exactly right, and have just finished the rough draft of an 8,000-word story in two days. It nearly slew me. As a rule, I find a week long enough for a short story, if I have the plot well thought out. I don't know if this new system is a good one or not. I shall probably go back to the old snail pace.

(2) On a novel I generally do eight pages a day, i.e., about 2,500 words, but I read the stuff over all the time and do endless rewriting.

(3) Recently I have had a great time with my work. We have been snowed up here after a record blizzard and nobody has been able to get at me for ages. The only catch was that we ran out of food and the last day all we could give Sammy for his dinner was a bit of bacon rind. I can still see his reproachful eye rolling up at me. It was a great moment when Loretta, our maid, suddenly ap-peared, dragging a sled loaded with provisions.

I must get hold of Alec Waugh's *The Loom of Youth*, that you speak so highly of. I've heard a lot about it. He must be pretty gifted to do anything big at seventeen. I was practically an imbecile at that age.

We sail on the "Adriatic" on April 24, as follows: Ethel carrying the black kitten, followed by myself with parrot in cage and Loretta following me with any other birds or animals we may acquire in the meantime. We shall have to leave Sammy behind, worse luck, owing to the quarantine laws. We shall miss him sorely, but fortunately it won't break his heart being parted from us, as he is the friend of all the world and can be happy with anybody. He cost us a fortune when we first had him, because he was always liking the looks of passersby outside our garden gate and trotting out and following them. The first time he disappeared we gave the man who brought him back ten dollars, and this got around among the local children and stirred up their business instincts. They would come to our gate and call "Sammy, Sammy, Sammy," and out old Sam would waddle, and then they would bring him back with a cheery "We found your dog wandering around down the road, mister," and cash in. I may add that the bottom has dropped out of the market and today any child who collects twenty-five cents thinks he has done well.

Arrandale Avenue
Great Neck
April 11, 1920

Dear Bill,

Just been down with lumbago. I went to an osteopath and he cured me all right, but he practically tore me limb from limb and I'm not at all sure that all of me is still there. I wonder what an osteopath does if a patient suddenly comes apart. ("Quick, Watson, the Scotch tape.")

That's terrific news about your breaking into the *Post* with "Bolshevik." And I'm tremendously impressed by their giving you

$600 for it. It's a most unusual thing for them to unbelt to that extent. I remember Lorimer telling me that he had paid $200 for Bozeman Bulger's latest story—what's become of Bulger, by the way? I haven't seen his name about for some time—and that very soon he would raise him to $250. He seemed to think that lavish. For a long time my short stories in the *Post* only fetched $400, so evidently Lorimer must have been hard hit by "Bolshevik." I don't wonder. It's a great story.

Listen, Bill. Is this a crazy idea? I suddenly thought the other day that, as there are always a lot of rats on a tramp ship, why shouldn't one rat, starting by being a good bit bigger than the other rats and so able to eat them daily, gradually grow and grow till he became the size of a bloodhound? This accomplished, he begins to throw his weight about. Mysterious things happen on the ship. The bosun is found dead with his face chewed off, two cabin boys disappear entirely. And so on. Is this any good to you? It certainly isn't to me. I would have to make the rat trip on a banana skin or try to touch the skipper for a fiver.

There really ought to be some sort of central bureau, an Ideas Exchange, where authors could send plots they couldn't use themselves and other authors could buy anything that suited their style. Thomas Hardy thinks of something on the lines of *Three Men in a Boat*. No good to him, but just right for Jerome K. Jerome, who buys it and sends the bureau the skeleton outline of a story about Wessex peasants getting hanged in Dorchester jail, which is right up Hardy's street and well worth what he has to pay for it. The bureau would charge ten per cent for its services and clean up.

Here's another one for you. Mate of ship murders captain to get his job, sets fire to ship to destroy all traces, takes crew ashore in open boat, becomes a hero and lives happily ever after—except for the moment when the captain's ghost comes and breathes down the back of his neck just as he is addressing his old school on How to Succeed.

Bill Townend wrote the rat story and it was published in *Harper's Magazine*, but it is not often that other people's plots are of much use to authors. I have had very little luck that way myself. Doing the sort of stuff I do, it is mostly from Schizophrenics that I receive these offers of assistance, and if I were to avail myself of them, it would not be long before an alienist was round at my address, instructing men in white coats to sit on my head while he adjusted the straitjacket. In the sixty years since I left the Hong Kong and Shanghai Bank I have written ten books for boys, one book for children, forty-seven novels, if you can call them novels, four hundred and sixty-nine articles, and three hundred and fifteen short stories, and only two of the novels and two of the short stories were not my own unaided work. The novels were based on plays by Guy Bolton and George S. Kaufman, the short stories, "Uncle Fred Flits By" and "The Amazing Hat Mystery," both with plots supplied by W. Townend.

Even apart from his triumphant entry into the *Saturday Evening Post*, Bill Townend got going as what is called a commencing author much more quickly than I have done. He sold his stories from the start, but during my two years in the bank all I got out of my literary efforts was a collection of rejection slips, and what I have always felt about rejection slips is that their glamour soon wears off. When you have seen one, you have seen them all.

The handicap under which most commencing authors struggle is that they don't know how to write. I was no exception to the rule. Worse bilge than mine may have been submitted to the editors of London in 1901 and 1902, but I should think it very unlikely. I was sorry for myself at the time when the stamped and addressed envelopes came homing back to me, but today my sympathy is for the unfortunate men who had to read my contributions. I can imagine nothing more depressing than being an editor and coming to the office on a rainy morning in February with a nail in one shoe and damp trouser legs and finding oneself confronted with six early Wodehouses—I used to send them out in batches of six—written, to make it more difficult, in longhand.

I was a quick worker in those days. In the summer of 1901 I contracted mumps and went home to have them in the bosom of my family. I was there three weeks, swelling all the time, and wrote twenty-one short stories, all of which, I regret, editors were compelled to reject owing to lack of space. The editors regretted it too. They said so.

My father had bought a house in Shropshire in 1900, and what I would have liked to do on leaving school was to dig in there and concentrate on the daily short story: but, placing this idea before my parents, I found them cold toward it. The cross all young writers have to bear is that, while they know they are going to be spectacularly successful some day, they find it impossible to convince their nearest and dearest that they will ever amount to a row of beans. Write in your spare time, parents say, and they pull that old one about literature being a good whatever-it-is, but a bad crutch.

The trouble in the Wodehouse home at the beginning of the century was that, while there was always a little something in the kitty for the butcher, the baker, and the groceryman, money was a good deal tighter than could have been wished. My father, after many years in Hong Kong, had retired on a pension, and the authorities paid it to him in rupees. A thoroughly low trick, in my opinion, for the rupee is the last thing in the world—or was then—with which anyone who valued his peace of mind would wish to be associated. It never stayed put for two weeks together. It was always jumping up and down and throwing fits, and expenditure had to be regulated in the light of what mood it happened to be in at the moment.

Its sudden plunge into the cellar having coincided with my last days at school, I do not blame my father for feeling that a son in a bank making his 80 pounds a year, just like finding it in the street, was a sounder proposition than one living at home and spending a fortune on stamps and envelopes. So Commerce got me, and Literature lost out for the time being.

Looking back, I don't think Literature missed much.

P.G.W.

4 *Onslow Square*
London
May 10, 1920

Dear Bill,

Yes, do send me any of your stories you feel doubtful about, and I'll do my best to tell you what, if anything, I think is wrong with them. Though, mark you, I've no claim to set myself up as an expert. I'm just a young fellow trying to get along by writing my sort of Gilbert the Filbert stuff, which seems to be going all right so far, and any advice I gave you about the quite different kind of thing you do might be all cockeyed. Still, an outsider can often spot something wrong which the writer has overlooked, so send them along.

I'll tell you one thing I believe one should never do, and that is destroy stuff one isn't satisfied with or stories which have had so many rejections that one's sick of the sight of them. One's always reading about authors who spend the morning at their desks and finish up by heaving a weary sigh and throwing all they've done into the wastepaper basket. I think they're crazy. You never know when some small bit in a story—just a line of dialogue, perhaps, or a description of a minor character—won't be exactly what you need later on to fit into another story. And there's always a chance that you may suddenly get an idea which will turn a dud story into a good one. I'm all against throwing away even the worst junk. Put it in the old chest, I say, just in case.

Why the ones you mention in your letter were rejected by so many editors I can't say, not having read them, but it may be that they were too good for the markets you sent them to. The pulps are fine when you're starting out and just trying to sell your stuff anywhere, but their tastes are pretty crude and I don't see how you can go on writing for them without deliberately making your work cheaper. I'd try to give them a miss in future, if you can manage it.

Your stories are about real people behaving as they would in real life. Take a thing like that one I thought was your very best, "In The Stokehold." It was all subtlety, and I was surprised that it got over with *Adventure*. You would have expected them to want something much more obvious. Not exciting enough, you'd have thought they would have said. It's the same with the English equivalents of the American pulps. Remember "The Luck Stone," which, with your assistance, I wrote for *Chums?* School story full of kidnapings, attempted murders, etc. They were delighted with it. Then I tried them with a real school story and they threw a fit. "What, no blood?" they cried, and shot the thing back at me.

I was thrilled and amused when, on rereading Plum's letters, I discovered by chance among them a note I had had from him, dated May 6, 1906. As follows:

> Dear Bill,
>
> Here's a go. I've been commissioned by *Chums* to do a 70,000-word serial by July. They want it not so public-schooly as the ones I've had in *The Captain* and with rather a lurid plot. For heaven's sake, rally round and lend a hand. Your reward will be my blessing and a fiver.

Though a fiver was a fiver in those days, Plum sent me ten pounds for the small amount of help I was able to give him. It should be of interest to any student of the works of P. G. Wodehouse to obtain the numbers of *Chums* for the latter part of 1906, if any still survive, and read *The Luck Stone* by—if I remember rightly—"Basil Windham."

W.T.

4 Onslow Square
London
June 27, 1922

Dear Bill,

I've just wired you that I think the story is great. The only criticism I would make is that, as a reader, I wished that your heavy had got it in the neck a bit more directly. Still, fine as it stands.

Listen, Bill, any funny plots you can send me will be heartily welcomed. I've got to start another series in the *Strand* soon and haven't any ideas except that I think I'll write some stories with Ukridge as the chief character. At the date of the series he is still unmarried and I can make him always in love with some girl or other, like Bingo Little, if necessary. The keynote is that he and his pals are all very hard up, and a plot which has as a punch Ukridge just missing touching someone for two bob would be quite in order.

I was hoping to send you what I've done of my new one, *Leave It to Psmith*, but there was something wrong with the layout and

I have had to start all over again after having written 30,000 words. This always happens to me unless I get my scenario right. I don't suppose I've ever done a 75,000-word novel that didn't involve writing 150,000 words, and always because the scenario had holes in it and I was satisfied with it too soon. I don't know how the big shots work their novels, but I make no pretense to being anything but a "popular" writer, and the first thing I have to do is to get a straight story line. You hear of novelists who invent a group of characters and then sit down and let them carry on as they see fit. I couldn't work that way. I wouldn't trust my characters an inch. If I sat back and let them take charge, heaven knows what the result would be. They have to do just what the scenario tells them to, and no funny business. It has always seemed to me that planning a story out and writing it are two separate things. If I were going to run a train, I would feel that the square thing to do was to provide the customers with railway lines and see that the points were in working order. Though, of course, that may hold good only for the action type of story, where you're building from situation to situation. Different, probably, if you were doing one of those psychological things.

In the case of *Leave It to Psmith* I think I shall have to put in another character. That often does the trick when you have an unsatisfactory layout.

Just got a cable from Ziegfeld, summoning me to America. He wants Guy and me to do a show for him. I shall be staying with Guy at Great Neck.

⁓⁓⁓

It is very seldom that an author gets handed anything on a plate, but I had this agreeable experience with Ukridge, which is pronounced Yewk-ridge, not Uck-ridge. One morning in 1905 I received a letter from Bill Townend in which he gave a long description of the vicissitudes undergone by an acquaintance of his named Craxton while trying to run a poultry farm in Devonshire. Bill started out in life as an artist, and he had the artist's eye for detail. The picture he gave me of Craxton—the optimism, the booming voice, the yellow mackintosh, and the ginger-beer–wired pince-nez—was so vivid that I felt I had known the man all my life, and it was almost without conscious cerebration that I wrote a novel called *Love among the Chickens,* the first thing I ever sold in America.

It was a pretty poor novel and fell with a dull thud when published in 1906, but since its republication in England in 1920 several hundred thousand splendid men and women have bought it, and more are lining up all the time with the price of admission clutched in their hot little hands. In America it ran serially in a magazine so long dead that I have forgotten its name, and was published in book form and also made into a silent movie. So, all in all, Ukridge had a reasonably successful debut.

The agent who handled the American deal was one of those up-and-coming but corkscrew-crooked literary agents who were common in 1906 but nonexistent today. Taking advantage of the fact that I was in England, three thousand miles away, he swiped the money for the serial, swiped the advance on the book, and in addition copyrighted the book in his name, so that when the movie was done, I had to pay him two hundred and fifty dollars to release the rights. He died shortly after that, not, in my opinion, a moment too soon.

P.G.W.

17 North Drive
Great Neck, N.Y.
December 16, 1922

Dear Bill,

Long time since I wrote, but what with one thing and another life has been pretty full.

On arriving in New York, we had a passing unpleasantness with the Customs people. Ethel had bought a necklace in London, and she filled up the form they give you to fill up before you land with "Nothing to Declare," and the Customs people decided that here was the jewel smuggler they had been waiting for so long. They spread the contents of her trunks all over the dock and even dug skewers into her cold cream. They told her she was "in serious trouble" and scared the pants off her.

I was off at one side talking to John Rumsey, my theatrical agent, who had come to meet the boat, and didn't for some time notice anything going on. Then I joined the group and asked what was up. They said Ethel had brought jewelry in and hadn't declared it. I said she didn't have to declare it, being just a visitor and not a resident, and the boss of the gang gave me a steely look and said, "I think you own a house in Great Neck, do you not?" "No," I said. "Ho!" he said. "Then why is your baggage labeled Great Neck?"

Do you remember the Scarlet Pimpernel, who was always flicking a speck of dust from the irreproachable mechlin lace at his wrists and looking down at people from beneath lazy eyelids? That was me. "It is labeled Great Neck," I said, flicking specks like nobody's business, "because we are about to enjoy the hospitality of Mr. Guy Bolton of 17 North Drive in that suburban resort. We sold our house a year ago." Well, you never saw such an apologetic activity. They had all Ethel's stuff packed again in two minutes flat, and after I had given them another look from beneath lazy eyelids, as much as to say "Don't let it happen again," we went on our way.

I've been swamped with work since I got here. We wrote the Ziegfeld musical comedy in two weeks, and it has been lying in a drawer ever since, Ziegfeld being busy with another production. This in spite of the fact that in his cable he said that every moment was precious. You never heard anything like the fuss he made when I told him I couldn't make the Wednesday boat but would sail on the Saturday. He gave me to understand that my loitering would ruin everything.

Working for Ziegfeld cuts both ways. You're pretty sure of a success and a lot of money, because anything he puts on is an Event and the customers roll up and buy seats just because it's a Ziegfeld show, but you have the feeling all the time that he regards book and lyrics as necessary evils and views them with concern. He has to have them, but he wishes he hadn't. His heart is with the Girls and their dresses. What he would like, if it could be done, would be to produce a thing where hundreds of lovely girls wandered in and out in gorgeous costumes and nobody said anything. He particularly dislikes comedy, and I don't blame him.

Since about the time of the Civil War he has been putting on the Ziegfeld Follies every year, full of star comedians who quarrel all the time and come running to him with their grievances, and this has given him a jaundiced outlook on that side of the business. I wouldn't call him a grouch exactly, but he's very grim and gloomy, unlike Charlie Dillingham, who is all joviality. I like him and get on very well with him. He often tells me he wishes he had my disposition (which, as you know, is sunny). He's darned lucky he hasn't, because if he had, he would never have been able to cope with those comedians. I would be wax in their hands. A man in his position needs to have the mentality of a lion tamer.

After putting the musical comedy in its drawer, I sat down to finish *Leave It to Psmith* and wrote 40,000 words in three weeks. Since then I have been working with Guy on a show for the Duncan Sisters, music by Irving Berlin. It is coming out slowly because Guy's new comedy has just started rehearsals and he is up to his neck in it and also because Irving is so elusive. All attempts to get hold of him about the music have failed. I went into New York last Monday to keep an appointment and found he had to rush off to his dentist. He then made a date with me over the phone to lunch with him on Thursday and work all the afternoon. I called at his apartment and he was out and had left no message. Heaven knows when the thing will ever be finished.

The *Post* has done me proud. Although they never commission anything, they liked the first 60,000 words of *Leave It to Psmith* so much that they announced it in the papers before I sent in the final chapters. I mailed them these on a Wednesday and got a check for $20,000 on the following Tuesday. Quick work.

The story will start in January, I think. Do you get the *Post* now? If not, let me know and I'll have it sent to you. I want you to cast your eye on the first installment in particular. I had a tremendous amount of plot to get across and I'd like you to see if I could improve the construction of it. I can't see any possible way of avoiding telling part of the story twice over, which is a nuisance, but I think it has come out pretty well.

What a problem it is to get a novel started just right. That business of introducing your characters and trying not to have them jostle one another and get in each other's way, and at the same time trying to make the damned thing readable. Particularly when you reflect that an editor probably makes up his mind about a story after reading Page One. Guy Bolton says the great thing in writing plays is never to give the audience too much to think about at any one time. In other words, in a play one mustn't try to develop two threads simultaneously, and this applies equally to stories. My besetting sin is a tendency to do all the exposition in one chunk on the first two pages instead of taking my time and spreading it out, and it generally takes me about six shots before I get the first five hundred words right.

Another profound observation of Guy's is "Get your love story set, and the comedy will take care of itself."

One thing I always try to do is to get to the dialogue as soon as possible on the first page of my typescript. Nothing puts the reader off more than a great slab of prose at the start. I was reading a short story of Booth Tarkington's the other day, and there were eleven pages of it before there was a line of dialogue. It was a good story when you got into it, but it would have been much easier going if there had been a bit of talk earlier. At least, that's how I feel. I'm like the woman who started to read Gibbon's *Decline and Fall of the Roman Empire* and didn't enjoy it because the pages were all alike and there was no conversation in them.

⌒〜⌒

Psmith, like Ukridge, was to a certain extent drawn from life. A cousin of mine who had been at school with Rupert D'Oyly Carte, the son of the Savoy Operas' D'Oyly Carte, was telling me one day about his eccentricities—how he was very long and lean, very well dressed, wore a monocle, and when one of the masters asked him, "How are you, Carte?," replied, "Sir, I get thinnah and thinnah." It gave me enough to build the character on, and I wrote a boys' story called "Mike" (1909), in which he figured largely. He continued his activities in *Psmith in the City* (1910), where he was a clerk in the New Asiatic Bank, an institution bearing a close resemblance to the Hong Kong and Shanghai Bank which I had joined in 1900.

It was very soon after he had entered their employment that the management of the New Asiatic Bank arrived at the conclusion that in adopting the life of commerce, Psmith had not found his niche and would be well advised to try some other walk in life: and with equal celerity the big shots of the Hong Kong and Shanghai Bank reached precisely the same conclusion about me. Either because I was a dedicated literary artist with a soul above huckstering or—which was the view more widely held in the office—because I was a plain dumb brick, I proved to be the most inefficient clerk whose trouser seat ever polished the surface of a high stool.

I was all right as long as they kept me in the postal department, where I had nothing to do but stamp and mail letters, a task for which my abilities well fitted me, but when they took me out of there and put me in Fixed Deposits, the whisper went around Lombard Street: "Wodehouse is at a loss. He cannot cope."

If there was a moment in the course of my banking career when I had the foggiest notion of what it was all about, I am unable to recall it. From Fixed Deposits I drifted to Inward Bills and from there to Outward Bills and Cash, always with a weak, apologetic smile on my face and hoping that suavity of manner would see me through when, as I knew must happen ere long, I fell short in my mystic duties. My total inability to grasp what was going on made me something of a legend in the place. Years afterwards, when the ineptness of a new clerk was under discussion in the manager's sanctum and the disposition of those present was to write him down as the worst bungler who had ever entered the Hong Kong and Shanghai Bank's portals, some white-haired veteran in charge of one of the departments would murmur, "No, no, you're wrong there. Young Robinson is, I agree, pretty subhuman, but you should have seen P. G. Wodehouse. Ah, they don't make them like that nowadays. They've lost the pattern."

Only two things connected with the banking industry did I really get into my head. One was that from now on all I would be able to afford for lunch would be a roll and butter and a cup of coffee, a discovery which, after the lavish meals of school, shook me to my foundations. The other was that if I was late in getting to the office oftener than three times a month, I would forfeit my Christmas bonus. One of the great sights in the City of London in the years 1901-1902 was me rounding into the straight with my coattails flying and my feet going pitter-patter-pat and just making it across the threshold, while thousands cheered. It kept me in splendid condition and gave me a rare appetite for the daily roll and butter.

P.G.W.

Dear Bill,

Yesterday morning I had a letter from Hoffman with the welcome news that he was buying your novel, *The Tramp,* for *Adventure*. I was very relieved, as I had been worrying. I felt that if he rejected it after you had sweated twelve weeks over it, you might turn your face to the wall and swear never to do a long story again. It's bad enough to have to write 80,000 words even when you're reasonably sure you have a market for them, but doing it on spec is absolute hell. What it must have been like in the three-volume-novel days, when they expected at least 200,-000 words from you, I can't imagine.

On the other hand, the longer the story, the more room you have for developing your characters. Much to be said on both sides, in fact.

Arnold Bennett insists that novels are the things to go for. In *How to Become an Author* he says: "He [the author] should take care to produce books at regular short intervals. He may continue this process for years without any really striking result in fame or money, and he may pessimistically imagine that his prolonged labors are fruitless. And then newspapers will begin to refer to him as a known author, as an author the mention of whose name is sufficient to recall his productions, and he will discover that all the while the building of his reputation has been going on like a coral reef. . . . But it must never be forgotten that while the reputation is being formed, the . . . public needs continuous diplomatic treatment. It must not be permitted to ignore his existence. At least once a year, and oftener if possible, a good solid well-made book should be flung into the libraries."

I don't agree when he advises against "frittering away energy on a lot of small things—e.g. short stories," but I think he's right about the necessity of turning out novels. It must have been especially so in the eighties and nineties, when magazines didn't print the names of contributors, because that was the only way of making a reputation. Life must have been pretty tough for magazine writers in those days of anonymity. I once saw a copy of *Beeton's Christmas Annual* for 1887, in which the first Sherlock Holmes story, "A Study in Scarlet," appeared. Not a mention of A. Conan Doyle. Just "A Reprint from the Reminiscences of John H. Watson, M.D., late of the Army Medical Department."

I am halfway through mapping out a new novel, *Bill the Conqueror*. I'm going on a new system this time, making the scenario very full, putting in atmosphere, dialogue, etc., so that when I come actually to write it the work will be easy. So far I have scenarioed out to about the 40,000-word mark, and it has taken me 13,000 words to do it. I have now reached a point where deep thought is required. I'm not sure I haven't got too much plot, and may have to jettison the best idea in the story. I suppose the secret of writing is to go through your stuff till you come on something you think is particularly good, and then cut it out.

Easthampton
Long Island
July 23, 1924

Dear Bill,

I have at last got the *Strand* with your "A Couple of Down-and-Outs" in it. I think the illustrations are good and the story reads fine. It has given me an illuminating idea about your work, and that is that you make your characters so real that, if you're writing for the popular magazines, you can't afford a gray ending. You simply must make a point of having things all right in the end, or the editor won't risk having his readers' feelings harrowed. Another thing is that what you want to put your stuff over is action. In "A Couple of Down-and-Outs" the story jumps from one vivid scene to another, whereas in some of the ones you've sent me it doesn't. The more I write, the more I am convinced that the only way to write a popular story is to split it up into scenes and have as little stuff in between as possible. And you can make a scene of almost anything. For instance, I wrote a Ukridge story the other day—"The Return of Battling Billson"—in which the only thing actually arrived at in the first thousand words was that I met Billson down in the East End and gave him Ukridge's address, which he had lost. It could have been done in half a dozen lines, but by making me go into a pub and get a drink and find I had had my pocket picked and so couldn't pay for it and be chucked out by the barman and picked up by Billson, who happened to be passing, and then having Billson go in and clean up the pub and manhandle the barman, I got a good comic scene which, I think—hope, anyway—quite concealed the fact that nothing had really happened except my giving him the address. (Though, of course, it did, I suppose, establish Billson's character.)

I'm glad you like the Ukridge series. I have done two more stories in the past three weeks. I found it difficult at first having the fellow who's telling the story a straight character and not a sort of Bertie Wooster, but now I find it rather a relief, as it seems to make the thing more real.

I think Hoffman's criticism of the other story you sent me was sound enough from his viewpoint. It's a very good story and ought to sell all right to one of the higher type magazines, but it was too gray for *Adventure*. You had your characters struggling against Life and Fate and all that sort of thing, and what *Adventure* wants are stories about men struggling with octopuses and pirates. The *Adventure* public don't like to feel uneasy and to have to say to themselves, "Well, maybe this fellow has got by this time, but what a wretched thought it is that the world is full of poor devils on the brink of being chucked out of jobs and put on the beach." You make them think about life, and popular magazine readers don't want to.

Another thing is that with that sort of story you eliminate any chance of comedy. Your hero can't approach his difficulties gaily and meet them in a dashing way. What I mean is, a man trapped in a ruined mill by pockmarked Mexicans and one-eyed Chinamen can be lively and facetious, whereas a man in the position of the hero of this story can't be anything but dead serious. This tends to make the thing heavy. But don't overlook the possibility (probability?) that I may be quite wrong about this. I don't really know anything about writing anything except farcical comedy. So if you come back at me with "There are nine-and-sixty ways of constructing tribal lays and every single one of them is right," I shan't have a word to say. I shall just redden and shuffle my feet.

Talking of one-eyed Chinamen, did I tell you that a man came up to me the other day and said, "Mr. Wodehouse, I want to thank you for the happy hours you have given me with your book *Fifty Years in China*"? It startled me a bit. I know working in the theater ages one a good deal, but, dash it, I'm only forty-one and the author of a book with a title like that would have to be at least seventy-five. I suppose it was the dark circles under my eyes that misled him.

⌁⌁⌁

I am writing these in-between-the-letters notes in 1961, and it will seem strange to my readers, if any, that I should have advised Bill Townend to attempt comedy, for today the humorist is certainly not the man most likely to succeed. He is like the dove sent out from the Ark which could find no parking place. Editors look askance at him and publishers view him with concern.

It was not so in the 1920s. In quantity and quality American humor led the world. You couldn't throw a brick in Times Square—not, of course, that one ever did—without hitting a whimsical novelist or a writer of what Thurber calls short nervous pieces. We had George Ade, Robert Benchley, Will Cuppy, Clarence Day, Will Rogers, Frank Sullivan, Oliver Herford, Ring Lardner, Don Marquis, F. P. Adams, Irvin Cobb, Harry Leon Wilson, Thorne Smith, and a thousand more. Life was one long giggle.

In these gray modern times you hardly ever see a funny story in the magazines, and in the theater it is even worse. Playwrights nowadays are writing nothing but that grim, stark stuff, and as about ten out of every twelve plays produced perish in awful agonies, I don't think they have the right idea. If only the boys would stop being so frightfully powerful and significant and give us a little comedy occasionally, everything would get much brighter. I am all for incest and tortured souls in moderation, but a good laugh from time to time never hurt anybody.

33

And nobody has laughed in a Broadway theater for years. All you hear is the soft, sibilant sound of creeping flesh, punctuated now and then by a sharp intake of the breath as somebody behind the footlights utters one of those four-letter words hitherto confined to the cozy surroundings of the lower type of barroom. (Odd to reflect, by the way, that when the word "damn" was first spoken on the New York stage—in one of Clyde Fitch's plays, if I remember rightly—there was practically a riot. Police raided the joint, and I'm not sure the military were not called out.)

Even in the musicals you never get a comedian now. The race seems to have died out, and I am convinced that the public misses them. I believe audiences want comedy, but dramatists won't let them have it. They are like stern nurses trying to make reluctant children take their spoonful of sulphur and molasses. "Why can't we have ice cream?" audiences plead, but the dramatists are firm. "Ice cream is not powerful and significant," they say. "Ice cream has no social message." Silly business all around, it seems to me, for what the nurses forget is that the kids are expected to unbelt $8.60 per spoonful and are at liberty to go and spend it elsewhere, which they do.

The process of getting back to comedy would, of course, be very gradual. At first a laugh during the progress of a play would have rather an eerie effect. People would wonder where the noise was coming from and would speculate as to whether somebody was having some sort of fit, but they would get into the way of it after a while, and it would not be so very long before it would be quite customary to see audiences looking and behaving not like bereaved relatives at a wake but as if they were enjoying themselves.

Over in Europe the humorous dramatist seems, from what one can gather, to be given a squarer deal, and there is no disposition to beat him over the head with a baseball bat if he offers the clientele something lighthearted. Whether this is because the European public is less sensitive, or because they have no baseball bats, remains a moot point, but it is a fact that farces which would barely survive a single night on Broadway run for years in London, and it is pretty generally recognized that only by setting your teeth and buckling down to it with iron determination can you write anything unfunny enough to fail in Paris.

If you ask me, I think we ought to bring the population of Paris over here, teach them English, and dump them down within easy reach of Forty-fifth Street. Then we should get somewhere.

In the sixteenth century they called humor "a disorder of the blood," and though they were probably just trying to be nasty, it is not a bad description. It is, anyway, a disorder of something. To be a humorist, one must see the world out of focus. You must, in other words, be slightly cockeyed. This leads you to ridicule established institutions, and as most people want to keep their faith in established institutions intact, the next thing that happens is that you get looked askance at. Statistics show that 87.03 of today's askance looks are directed at humorists, for the solid citizenry suspect them and are wondering uneasily all the time what they are going to be up to next, like baby-sitters with charges who are studying to be juvenile delinquents. There is an atmosphere of strain such as must have prevailed long ago when the king or prince or baron had one of those Shakespearean Fools around the castle, capering about and shaking a stick with a bladder and little bells attached to it. Tradition compelled him to employ the fellow, but nothing was going to make him like it.

"Never can understand a word that character says," he would mutter peevishly to his wife as the Fool went capering about the throne room, jingling his bells. "Why on earth do you encourage him? It was you who started him off this morning. All that nonsense about crows!"

"I only asked him how many crows can nest in a grocer's jerkin. Just making conversation."

"And what was his reply? Tinkling like a xylophone, he gave that awful cackling laugh of his and said, 'A full dozen at cockcrow, and something less under the dog star, by reason of the dew, which lies heavy on men taken with scurvy.' Is that a system? Was that sense?"

"It was humor."

"Who says so?"

"Shakespeare says so."

"Who's Shakespeare?"

"All right, George."

"I never heard of any Shakespeare."

"I said all right, George. Skip it."

"Well, anyway, you can tell him from now on to keep his humor to himself, and if he hits me on the head just once more with that bladder of his, he does so at his own risk. He's always hitting me on the head with his bladder. Every time he gets within arm's reach of me—socko! And for that I pay him a penny a week, not deductible. He makes me sick."

Humorists as a class are gloomy men, and it is this sense of being apart from the herd, of being, as one might say, the poison-ivy rash on the body politic, that makes them so, though they have other troubles as well. As that notable humorist E. B. White says, they are looked down on by the critics, regarded as outside the pale of literature, and seldom recognized as possessing talents worth discussing. People are very serious today, and the writer who refuses to take them seriously is viewed with concern and suspicion.

"Fiddle while Rome burns, would you?" they say to him, and treat him as an outcast.

I think we should all be sorry for humorists and try to be very kind to them, for they are so vulnerable. You can blot the sunshine from their lives in an instant by telling them you don't see what there is so funny in *that*, and if there is something funny in it, you can take all the heart out of them by calling them facetious or describing them as "mere" humorists. A humorist who has been called mere can never be quite the same again. He frets. He refuses to eat his cereal. He goes about with his hands in his pockets and his lower lip jutting out, kicking stones and telling himself that the life of a humorist is something that ought not to happen to a dog, which of course in many ways is substantially true.

The most melancholy humor today is, of course, the Russian, and one can readily understand why. If you live in a country where, when winter sets in, your nose turns blue and parts from its moorings, it is difficult to be rollicking, even when primed with two or three stiff vodkas. Khrushchev probably would be considered Russia's top funnyman—at least, if you were domiciled in Moscow and didn't feel that way, you would do well to keep it to yourself—and he has never got beyond the Eisenhower golf joke and the Russian proverb; and if there is anything less hilarious than a Russian proverb, we have yet to hear of it. The only way to laugh at one is to watch Khrushchev and see when he does it.

"In Russia," says Khrushchev, making his important speech to the Presidium, "we have a proverb—A chicken that crosses the road does so to get to the other side, but wise men dread a bandit," and then his face sort of splits in the middle and his eyes disappear into his cheeks like oysters going down for the third time in an oyster stew, and the comrades realize that this is the big boffola and that if they are a second late with the belly laugh, their next job will be running a filling station down Siberia way.

There may come a time when Russia will rise to He-and-She jokes and stories about two Irishmen who were walking up Broadway, but I doubt it. I cannot see much future for Russian humorists. They have a long way to go before they can play the Palace.

Oddly, considering that humor is so despised, people are always writing articles or delivering lectures about it, generally starting off with the words "Why do we laugh?" (One of these days someone is going to say "Why shouldn't we?" and they won't know which way to look.) Here is what Dr. Edmund Bergler says in his book on *The Sense of Humor:*

> Laughter is a defense against a defense. Both maneuvers are instituted by the subconscious ego. The cruelty of the superego is counteracted by changing punishment into inner pleasure. The superego reproaches the ego for the inner pleasure, and the ego then institutes two new defenses, the triad of the mechanism of orality and laughter.

What do you mean, you don't know what he means? Clear as crystal. Attaboy, Edmund. Good luck to you, and don't laugh at any wooden nickels.

P.G.W.

Easthampton
Long Island
August 9, 1924

Dear Bill,

I have the honor to report that the old bean is in a state of absolute stagnation. I wrote the best golf story I have ever done on the boat coming over—"The Coming of Gowf"—but since I landed I haven't had the ghost of an idea for a plot of any kind—so much so—or so little so—that I shall be obliged to drop the Ukridge series—at any rate for the moment—at the end of the ninth story. I wanted the last two stories to be about how he got married, and it looked as if it would be pretty easy, but I'm darned if I can think of anything for him to do. It may come later. I've done a lot of work this year—twelve short stories and half a novel, besides my share of *The Beauty Prize*, including all the lyrics—and it may simply be that I need a rest.

The kitten has had a fit but is all right again now. I allude to the animal at the Wodehouse home at Easthampton, whom you have never met. A cheery soul, with a fascinating habit of amusing the young master at breakfast by chasing a ball of paper all over the room and then suddenly dashing up the curtain from floor to ceiling at one bound. Sammy, the bulldog, has had an attack of eczema but is doing well. No other news except that yesterday I was knocked down by a car. Have you ever been knocked down by a car? If not, avoid the experience. There's no percentage in it. I was strolling along to meet Ethel, who had gone to the station in our Buick, and halfway to the village she sighted me and pulled in toward the sidewalk. The roads here are cement, with a sort of no-man's-land of dirt between sidewalk and road. I had just got to this when I saw a Ford coming down behind our car. I naturally thought it would pull up when the driver saw that Ethel had stopped, so I continued to stand in the no-man's-land, and I suddenly observed with interest that it wasn't even thinking of stopping but was swinging in straight for me at about sixty miles an hour, cutting round Ethel on the right. I gave one gazelle-like spring sideways and the damned thing's front wheel caught me squarely on my left leg as I was in midair. I took the most awful toss and came down on the side of my face and broke my glasses and skinned my nose, my leg, and my right arm. This morning all sorts of unsuspected muscles and bones are aching and the whole of the inside of my left thigh is a bright purple. Just goes to show that we are here today and gone tomorrow, doesn't it? If I had been a trifle less fit and active and not so able to soar through the air with the greatest of ease, I should have got the entire car in the wishbone. The driver was a kid of about fifteen. He said he was sorry, and I said, "Don't mention it," and we parted with mutual civilities.

Last night I went to bed early and read your story "Peter the Greek." For the first half I thought it was the best thing you had done, full of action and suspense. But, honestly, as you seem to think yourself from your letter, it does drop rather badly after that. It "needs work," as they keep telling you when you're out on the road with a show. I spotted one small point. Mogger, your Heavy, is established as no end of a tough guy, and you have him knocked down by Teame, who is quite a minor character. You shouldn't ever have your villain manhandled by anyone except the hero. Just imagine Professor Moriarty socked by Dr. Watson or, for the matter of that, by Mrs. Hudson the landlady. A heavy ought to be a sort of scarcely human, apparently invulnerable figure. You want the reader to be in a constant state of panic, saying to himself, "How the devil is this superman to be foiled?" If he gets knocked base over apex by one of the bit players, this feeling of awe is weakened.

And another thing. I've spoken of this before and I want to emphasize it again. You *must not* take any risk of humanizing your villains in a story of action. And by humanizing I mean treating them subjectively and not objectively. Taking Moriarty as the pattern villain, don't you see how much stronger he is by being an inscrutable figure and how much he would have been weakened if Conan Doyle had done a chapter showing his thoughts? A villain ought to be a sort of malevolent force, not an intelligible person. You don't want to get inside him at all, only to have him seen through the eyes of other people.

I wish we could meet and talk these things over. It's so hard to discuss a story by correspondence. The time to wrangle over construction is when the thing is being shaped, not after it has set.

I'm sailing for England next Friday for the rehearsals of *The Beauty Prize* at the Winter Garden, so we shall be able to get together, but make it snappy, as I shall be going back to New York at the end of three weeks, possibly sooner. You remember me telling you about that show for the Duncan Sisters, with music by Irving Berlin? It's starting rehearsals in three weeks, but not with Irving's music. It's a good instance of the sort of trouble you run into in the theater. What happened was that we didn't plan to produce till the autumn and the Duncans asked Sam Harris, our manager, if they could fill in during the summer with a little thing called *Topsy and Eva*, a sort of comic *Uncle Tom's Cabin* which they had written themselves. They just wanted to do it for a short run in Chicago, they said. Sam said that would be all right, so they went ahead, expecting to play a month or so, and darned if *Topsy and Eva* didn't turn out to be one of those colossal hits which run forever. It's now in about its fiftieth week in Chicago, with New York still to come. So we lost the Duncans and, owing to losing them, lost Sam Harris and Irving Berlin, who thought the thing wouldn't go without the Duncans. So we got hold of Jerry Kern for the music, and Ray Comstock, who did our Princess Theatre shows, is putting it on. Jerry has done a fine score, as always, but the thing was written as a vehicle for a sister act and I doubt if we can get by without the Duncans. The best thing about the show is its title, *Sitting Pretty*.

～ ⁓ ～

Sitting Pretty came off after a short run, the only one of the six Bolton-Wodehouse-Kern musical comedies that did not play a whole season in New York.

W.T.

～ ⁓ ～

Looking back after forty years, in the riper wisdom of 1961, I can see that we ought to have realized from the start that *Sitting Pretty* hadn't a hope. It don't add up right, as Abe Erlanger used to say. With the Duncans in mind, we had made the two sisters children, because that was what the Duncans liked to be. At the rise of the curtain they were in an orphanage, and nothing to suggest that they are more than ten or eleven years old. Yet scarcely is the opening chorus over when both are deep in a couple of love affairs, which culminate at eleven P.M. in a double wedding. It just wouldn't do. Audiences may be asses, but they are not silly asses, and there was none of that "willing suspension of disbelief" of which the poet Coleridge speaks. Disbelief was, on the contrary, rife, and we closed Saturday.

It is curious, though, how every now and then the customers will accept something that is completely unbelievable. In Gilbert and Sullivan's *H. M. S. Pinafore* Captain Corcoran has a daughter who, one presumes, is twenty-three or so. She falls in love with Ralph Rackstraw, the sailor, who can't be more than twenty-five. The Captain, as the father of a girl of that age, can hardly be less than forty-five, more probably fifty. And the big surprise at the final curtain is Little Buttercup's revelation that the Captain and Ralph were left in her charge as babies and

Oh, bitter is my cup!
    However could I do it?
I mixed those children up,
    And not a creature knew it!

Pinafore was produced in 1878 and is still going strong, nobody seeming to have noticed that it don't add up right.

P.G.W.

Great Neck, N.Y.
September 24, 1924

Dear Bill,

Ethel has gone back to England to get us a London house, while I stay on here for a week or two to finish an adaptation of a Hungarian play for Gilbert Miller.

Adaptations are pie, but I don't believe I could ever do a play of my own. It's a special knack which seems to come to Guy naturally but has eluded me. We are supposed to be collaborators, but in actual practice he does all the work on the book, while I look in from time to time and say, "How are you getting on?" Giving the thing the Wodehouse touch, you might say. Still, I do do the lyrics, so I suppose I'm entitled to my royalties.

The first play I was ever connected with was a collaboration with a boy named Henry Cullimore when I was seven. I don't know what made us decide to do it, but we did, and Henry said we would have to have a plot. "What's a plot?" I asked. He didn't know. He had heard or read somewhere that a plot was of the essence, but as to what it was he confessed himself fogged. This naturally made us both feel a little dubious as to the outcome of our enterprise, but we agreed that there was nothing to do but carry on and hope that everything would pan out all right. (Chekhov used to do this.)

He—Henry Cullimore, not Chekhov—was the senior partner in the project. He was three years older than I was, which gave him an edge, and he had a fountain pen. I mostly contributed

41

moral support, as with Guy Bolton, but, unlike Guy, Henry let me down. He got as far as

ACT ONE
(*Enter Henry*)
HENRY: What's for breakfast? Ham and oatmeal?
Very nice.

But there he stopped. He had shot his bolt, and, as I had nothing to suggest, we called the thing off.

How he was planning to go on if inspiration hadn't blown a fuse, I never discovered. I should imagine that the oatmeal would have proved to be poisoned—("One of the barbiturate group, Inspector, unless I am greatly mistaken")—or a dead body would have dropped out of the closet where they kept the sugar.

I meant this letter to be about your *The Talking Doll*, but I'll have to wait a day or two, as I haven't been able to read it yet.

Great Neck, N.Y.
September 29, 1924

Dear Bill,

About *The Talking Doll*, which I have just finished. It gripped me all through except at the very end. If you are going to start anything in a story like the idea of Chutton and the talking doll—supernatural stuff—it's brutal to the reader to explain it away in the last chapter. It's like the ghost turning out to be smugglers. A supernatural story ought to be supernatural all through.

Another thing. I think you have made a mistake in starting interesting stuff and then dropping it, so that a character who looks as if he were going to develop into importance fades out. The principle I always go on in writing a novel is to think of the characters in terms of actors in a play. I say to myself, when one of them has showed up strongly in an early scene: "If this were a musical comedy, we should have to get somebody with a big name to play this part, and if he found that he had practically nothing to do in the second act, he would walk out. Now, then, can I twist the story so as to give him plenty to do all the way through?" A good instance of what I mean was Baxter in *Leave It to Psmith*. It became plain to me as I constructed the scenario that Baxter had become established as such an important character that he simply had to have a big scene toward the end of the book, so I bunged in that flowerpot sequence.

The one thing actors—important actors, I mean—won't stand for is having their parts fade out in the second and third acts, and I believe this isn't vanity but is based on an instinctive knowledge of stagecraft. They kick because they know the balance isn't right.

I wish we could discuss these stories before you finish them. It's so much easier to see where a scenario goes off the rails. If one has finished a long story, one goes cold on it. I had this experience with *Leave It to Psmith*. You and a number of other people told me the end was wrong, as I had already suspected myself, but I couldn't muster up energy and ideas enough to fix it. I finally did, and it's all right now, I think, but it was like trudging along a dusty road with blisters on both feet.

* * *

I suppose there is nothing that makes an author pick at the coverlet more feverishly than this business of having his characters become so major that it is impossible to use them in one early sequence and then drop them. It has often been attempted, but never with success. Dickens tried it in *Master Humphrey's Clock*. He brought on Mr. Pickwick and Sam Weller at the beginning of that work and had them play a scene, and the result was terrible. He very wisely scrapped the book. Kipling introduced Stalky as a subsidiary character in a short story, and he fell as flat as a Dover sole. In a novel which I am planning out at this moment I have an opening chapter in which I would love to bring on Bertie Wooster's Aunt Dahlia for a single scene—she would make all the difference to the thing—but I can't do it, as there is nothing else for her in the story. You can't have a star actor come on at eight fifty-three, just as half the audience are shuffling into their seats, and go off for the night at eight fifty-nine.

The first thing an author has to realize is that a major character is a major character is a major character, as Gertrude Stein would say.

P.G.W.

43

Dear Bill,

We have taken this house for a year, though I never expect to stay a year in any one spot these days. How is your cottage working out? One thing about living in the country is that, even if the roof leaks, you can get some writing done. I find it's the hardest job to get at the stuff here, as we have so many lunches and dinners which just eat up the time. If I have a lunch hanging over me, it kills my morning's work, and dinner isn't much better. I hate the social life. My dream would be to live in the country with a typewriter and plenty of paper and tobacco and be cut by the county.

I'm mapping out a new novel—title, *Sam in the Suburbs*—the action starting in America and going on to Dulwich, and I enclose a list of questions, which you will save my life by answering. My hero goes from New York to London Dock on a tramp ship, and I am planning Chapter Three to start as follows: "Sam Shotter stood outside the galley of the tramp steamer 'Araminta' in pleasant conversation with Clarence ('Soup') Todhunter, the vessel's popular and energetic cook."

Now then:

(A) How was Sam dressed? (All his luggage had come over on the "Mauretania" and he has sea clothes on. This is very important, as in the next chapter it is essential that Sam shall look like a deadbeat, because it leads to various happenings.)

(B) Sam is a friend of the skipper, so that it's all right his being on board. But in what capacity did he sail? Would he have to have some definite job? They don't take passengers on tramps, do they?

(C) The "Araminta" would take how long for the voyage from America? How would Soup Todhunter be dressed? Can you give me some atmosphere for Port of London—i.e., something for Sam to see from the deck of the ship?

(D) I shall probably want a scene between Sam and the skipper, presumably in the latter's cabin, so what is the skipper doing when the boat has just docked? I mean, probably the boat is discharging cargo or has been during the day. I want Sam to get off the ship in nice time to take the skipper up to the West End for a bit of dinner, because that's when the plot starts to thicken.

(E) Sam, by the way, is the godson—original touch, that. You thought I was going to say nephew—of a shipowner. He is working in the firm, and his job involves going down to the docks at all sorts of unearthly hours to interview skippers of incoming tramps, which is how he comes to know the skipper of the "Araminta."

NOW! IS THERE SUCH A JOB?

Well, that's all I can think of at the moment. I'm keeping a carbon copy of these questions, so you'll only need to jot down notes under each heading. I do hope you're not too busy just now, as I don't want to interrupt you. Also bear in mind that I can carry on quite well for several weeks without the information. I have got the story so set that I can skip the Port of London stuff and work on the shore scenes till you're ready.

I answered all the questions with great care, but, alas, in the completed book Sam Shotter never did stand outside the galley of the tramp steamer "Araminta" in pleasant conversation with Clarence ("Soup") Todhunter. In the final version the meeting took place offstage and is merely referred to in the words "Sam had dined well, having as his guest his old friend Hash Todhunter"—not "Soup," an honorable name bestowed later on Mr. Slattery, the burglar in *Hot Water*. All I actually accomplished was to put Plum right about Sam's costume and Hash's looks. But that formidable list of questions shows the thoroughness with which he approached a job of work.

Plum was right about not staying a year in any one spot. Shortly after I received this letter, he went to New York to do a musical version of *The Three Musketeers* for Florenz Ziegfeld.

W.T.

45

Dear Bill,

I would have written before, but ever since I landed I have been in a terrific rush. I finished a rough version of the *Musketeers* on the boat, but, like all work that's done too quickly, it needed a lot of fixing. I was working on it when a fuse blew out in Ziegfeld's Marilyn Miller show—book by Guy Bolton and Bill McGuire—owing to the lyrist and the composer turning up on the day of the start of rehearsals and announcing that they had finished one number and hoped to get another done shortly, though they couldn't guarantee this.

After Flo had recovered from the fainting fit induced by this news, he postponed the *Musketeers*, fired the lyrist and composer of the Marilyn Miller show, and called in two new composers, Sigmund Romberg and George Gershwin, and asked me to do the lyrics with Ira Gershwin. Meanwhile, Gilbert Miller wanted an adaptation in a hurry for Irene Bordoni, so I started on that, too. By writing the entire second act in one day, I have managed to deliver the Bordoni show on time, and I have now finished my share of the lyrics of the Flo show, and all is well—or will be till Flo wants them all rewritten, as he is sure to do. We open the Bolton-McGuire-Ira Gershwin-Wodehouse-George Gershwin-Romberg effort in Boston next week. It's called *Rosalie*, and I don't like it much, though it's bound to be a success with Marilyn and Jack Donahue in it.

Just at present I feel as if I would never get another idea for a story. I suppose I shall, but this theatrical work certainly saps one's energies. As I write this, it is six o'clock, so the play I adapted for Ernest Truex, *Good Morning, Bill*, must just be finishing in London. I hope it has got over, as I know Gilbert is waiting to see how it is received in London before putting it on here.

New York is noisier than ever. I found my only way of getting any work done on the Flo lyrics was to take a room at the Great

Neck Golf Club and work there. So I became the only man on record who commuted the wrong way. I used to catch the twelve o'clock train from New York every day and return after dinner. Flo thought I played golf all day out there and was rather plaintive about it, but I soothed him by producing a series of lyrics.

⌁

Good Morning, Bill was a success. *Rosalie* turned out a credit to its platoon of authors, doing 335 performances at the New Amsterdam Theatre. Plum was later to undergo some headaches out in Hollywood, trying to turn it into a motion picture for Marion Davies.

W.T.

Hunstanton Hall
Norfolk
July 3, 1928

Dear Bill,

The above address doesn't mean that I have bought a country house; it's a joint belonging to a friend of ours, and I am putting in a week or two here. It's one of those enormous houses, about two-thirds of which are derelict. There is a whole wing which hasn't been lived in for half a century. You know the sort of thing—it's happening all over the country now—thousands of acres, park, gardens, moat, etc., but very little ready money. The income from farms and so on just about balances expenses.

I spend most of my time on the moat, which is really a sizable lake with a couple of islands in it. I'm writing this in the punt with my typewriter on a bed table. There is a duck close by which utters occasional quacks like a man with an unpleasant voice saying nasty things in an undertone. Beside me is a brick wall with the date 1623 on it. I wish I could settle down in a place like this instead of having to be always dashing about all over the world.

What a mine of copy these remote English districts are. Progress seems to have left them untouched. You'd think some of these

47

landowners were living in the eighteenth century, not the twentieth. Man who owns a place near here told his chauffeur to be at the front door at three sharp one afternoon to take him to a neighboring town, and the chauffeur didn't bring the car around till five minutes past the hour. Man says nothing, but at midnight that night he routs his butler out of bed and tells him to tell chauffeur that he wants the car immediately. Chauffeur, roused out of a deep sleep, puts on his uniform and brings the car to the door, and employer says, "All right, you can take it back now. I just wanted to impress on you that when I say three, I mean three, not five minutes past."

Another time, this fellow was expecting a friend of his from London. Friend telephones to say he will be late, as his car has broken down. Eventually arrives at two in the morning. What does he get when he clocks in? A drink and a sandwich? Not at all. Our hero once more routs butler out of bed, tells him to rouse cook, says guest must have a full dinner after his journey. So at three in the morning guest sits down to melon, clear soup, fish, pheasant with chipped potatoes and two veg, a soufflé, coffee, and liqueurs, with butler and footman in attendance, probably walking in their sleep.

The trouble is that I don't see how I could possibly use stuff like that in a story. Nobody would believe it. Why didn't the domestic staff resign in a body, as domestic staffs do these days at the drop of a hat? I don't know, but they didn't.

Hunstanton Hall
Norfolk
July 20, 1928

Dear Bill,

I liked both the stories you sent me and I'm sure they will sell all right. My only criticism is of the names of the characters. You certainly have thought up some pretty ghastly labels for the poor slobs . . . Overeck, Hawksweed, Negus, Hemlock, Ferrule,

Affleck, etc. . . . and what I'm kicking about is that they've *all* got names like that. Every single ruddy able-bodied seaman on board your ship has a name nobody ever heard of. It offends one's sense of probability. One feels that there couldn't be a ship's company that didn't have an occasional Smith, Jones, or Robinson in it.

Of course, you do get the most extraordinary names in real life, but the point I'm making is that minor characters ought not to have them or the reader gets misled. It's a mistake to give a minor character, someone who's just one of the chorus boys, so to speak, a name that suggests that he's going to be a major character. The reader unconsciously gets the feeling that a fellow wouldn't be called Weatherwax or Changlefeather or whatever it may be unless the author was drawing particular attention to him and planning to use him in some big situation later on, and when this doesn't happen he's disappointed.

Odd how important story names are. It always takes me about as long to get them to my satisfaction as it does to write the novel. Did you know that Conan Doyle originally intended to call Dr. Watson Ormond Sacker? It can't have taken him long to see that that was wrong. If you have a stolid, ordinary character, you have to give him a stolid, ordinary name. He could have called Holmes Ormond Sacker, though I wouldn't have recommended it, but not Watson. Sherlock Holmes, by the way, started out as Sherringford Holmes. Did you know that?

Conan Doyle, a few words on the subject of. Don't you find, as you get older, that the tragedy of life is that your early heroes lose their glamour? I mean, as a lad in the twenties you worship old whoever-it-is, the successful author, and think he's the greatest thing that ever happened, and by the time you're forty you find yourself blushing hotly at the thought that you could ever have admired the bilge he writes. Now, with Doyle I don't have this feeling. I used to think his stuff swell, and I still think it swell. Do you remember when we used to stand outside the bookstall at Dulwich station on the first of the month, waiting for it to open so that we could get the new *Strand* with the latest installment of Doyle's *Rodney Stone* . . . and the agony of finding that something had happened to postpone the fight between Champion Harrison and Crab Wilson for another month? (Incidentally, Harrison and Wilson, you notice, not Wasserback and Bodfish.)

Apart from his work, I admire Doyle so much as a man. He's so solid, and I loved that measured way he has of talking, like Sherlock Holmes. He was telling me once that when he was in America he saw an advertisement in a paper—"Conan Doyle's School of Writing. Let the Conan Doyle School of Writing teach you how to sell" or something to that effect. In other words, some crook was using his name to pull a fast one on the public. Well, what most people would have said in his place would have been "Hullo! Something fishy here." The way he put it when telling me the story was "I said to myself, 'Ha! There is villainy afoot.' "

Just had a cable saying the *Post* have taken *Fish Preferred* and are paying me $40,000, as they have been doing for the last two or three. My next job will be a serial which the *Cosmopolitan* have commissioned. They are giving me $50,000 for it. I'm going to do a novel-length Jeeves story, if I can think of a plot, though, these told-in-the-first-person things are always a bit tricky, as the reader can know nothing except what Bertie tells him and Bertie can know only a limited amount himself. But, of course, you can work up much more speed in a first-person story.

> *Hunstanton Hall*
> *Norfolk*
> *August 1, 1928*

Dear Bill,

A shadow has fallen on Hunstanton Hall (pronounced Hunston, in case you didn't know). Host has had a row with butler, who has given notice. This butler is a cheery soul who used to be the life of the party, joining in the conversation at meals as he handed the potatoes and laughing appreciatively if I made a joke, but now he hovers like a specter, very strong and silent. I'm hoping peace will be declared soon.

Glad to hear about your Gaumont deal. It ought to help the

sale of the book a lot. I went round to the Jenkins headquarters before I left London and had a long talk with Askew about your work, Grimsdick being away. He was very enthusiastic and said they thoroughly believed in you and thought your stuff fine and intended to stick to it and build you up. He realizes what I have always felt, that your sort of work has to be built up. Mine was just the same. I didn't sell over two thousand till I went to Jenkins with *Piccadilly Jim*. I don't think you can expect a big sale with an early book, unless it happens to be one of those freak winners. The thing to do is to bung in book after book with one publisher.

Do stick to Jenkins. The more I see of them, the more I think they are the best publishers this side of the Atlantic. Askew has been right through the bookselling business, starting as an apprentice, and this gives him a great advantage. Sometimes when I see those column ads of other publishers in the Sunday papers, I get rather wistful, but I always come back to feeling that the Jenkins people do much more for their authors than any of them. I mean to say, while these other blokes are buying column ads, Askew is going round and taking some bookseller whom he used to play marbles with out for a drink and landing him with a hundred copies of your book.

The only way to get a book public is to keep plugging away without any long intervals. They don't know you're writing till you've published about half a dozen. I produced five books which fell absolutely flat, and then got going with *Piccadilly Jim*. I suppose if *Piccadilly Jim* had been published first, it would have been just as much a flop as the others, but all the time I must have been creating a public bit by bit, and I feel it's going to be the same with you.

I've just read your Captain Crupper story in the *Strand*. Very good. You ought to do a lot more Crupper stories. "Such as?" you say. Well, did you read a thing of mine about Lord Emsworth and his pig called "Pig-hoo-o-o-o-ey"? The idea of it was that there was some perfectly trivial thing which was important to the principal character, and the story was about how he got it. But in the process of getting it he becomes entangled in somebody's love story and all sorts of things happen, but he pays no attention to them, being wholly concentrated on this small thing. You don't follow me? Well, Lord Emsworth was distracted because his pig wouldn't eat, and in the end, owing to the hero having been a hog caller in Nevada and so knowing how to coax pigs to the trough, it does eat. This leads to the hero getting the heroine, but Lord Emsworth doesn't care a damn about that, the important thing to him being that his pig has called off its fast and is once more digging in and getting its carbohydrates. I can see Crupper in the same sort of situation.

Did I tell you we have a new Peke—Susan? She adopted me from the start, and her devotion is beginning to affect my liver. I can't get any real exercise. She won't let me out of her sight, and she won't come for walks. What she likes is to lie in the middle of the lawn and have me walk round and round her. She won't let me go out in the punt on the moat, and if I bicycle to the town, I have to take her along, tucked into my sweater.

In the intervals of writing *The Small Bachelor* I'm working on an adaptation (for America) of a German play. When I was in New York, I was talking to Gilbert Miller, and Al Woods was there, and I said to G.M., "I wish you would give me Molnár's play to adapt." He said, "You couldn't do it. It's a serious play." I said, "Boy, I can write anything. Stand to one side and let me at it." Al Woods said, "I have a serious German play," and I said, "Gimme." So he gave it to me, and that's the one I'm working on now. I'll bet it'll be a historic flop, because of course I can't really write serious stuff, and why I ever let myself in for the damned thing, I can't imagine. I must have been cuckoo.

❦

The Al Woods play was not a flop, but only because it was never produced. Al took one look at my script and decided that the wise course was to forget about the whole thing.

The Small Bachelor—so titled because the hero lived in a small bachelor apartment in Greenwich Village—was based on *Oh, Lady! Lady!* the show Guy Bolton, Jerry Kern, and I did for the Princess in 1917. Turning a play into a novel is not as easy as it might seem. It is not just a matter of taking the lines of the play and putting in "he said" and "she said" after them, with a few "He turned pale's" and "She smiled roguishly's" in between. I had to invent additional characters and new situations or the opus would not have run to 30,000 words. I wrote 40,000 words before I reached the point where *Oh, Lady!* started. But of course, when I did get there, things eased greatly.

I have twice turned plays into novels. The other one was George S. Kaufman's *The Butter and Egg Man*, produced at the Longacre Theatre in 1925. The novel was called *Angel Cake* in America, *Barmy in Wonderland* in England. In the play the hero is a guileless young American from the Middle West who is talked by a tough Broadway manager into putting money into a production. I made him a guileless young Englishman, added several characters, and changed the heroine a good deal.

George and I split the proceeds fifty-fifty, and Scott Meredith, my agent, sent him his share of the advance. Two years later, he called Scott up on the telephone. "I've just found a check for $1,350 from you in an old pair of trousers. Could you tell me what it is for?" said George.

The book was published under my name, and the reviewer of the N. Y. *Times* was very nice about it, but he clicked his tongue in the final paragraph. He wrote:

"After all these years, by the way, Wodehouse has not learned to imitate colloquial American. His Broadway characters talk like Aaron Slick of Punkin Crick, which rather tends to spoil the effect."

Every single line of the Broadway characters' dialogue was Kaufman's, that recognized master of Broadway slang.

P.G.W.

17 Norfolk Street
London W. 1
November 12, 1928

Dear Bill,

This looks like being my permanent address. Ethel bought the house when I was at Hunstanton. It's a huge place just off Park Lane and we have a butler, a cook, a footman, two housemaids, a parlormaid, and a scullery maid, so I suppose I'm in for the social life again, which I hate. Not bad for work, though, if you can keep the British aristocracy away. I write all the morning, go for a five-mile walk after lunch, and can generally get in another three hours before dinner, as we don't dine till eight.

It's rather funny. You know when a cat's going to have kittens you fix up a cozy apartment for her with a warm blanket and all the trimmings, and then she goes and has them in a drafty corner of the cellar lying in the dark on damp stone. Much the same thing has happened with me. Ethel, bless her, was determined that I should have a really good place for my writing, so her first move was to furnish a large room on the first floor as a library—old books round the walls, luxurious chairs, a massive desk, etc.—and, of course, my first move was to go and do all my work in my bedroom on a kitchen table. Did you read a recent story in the *Post* about an author who could never write unless he was in the greatest discomfort? I remember that his masterpiece was turned out in a haunted house with strange groanings going on and doors opening silently without hands. I'm rather like that.

Do you read John Galsworthy's books? He came to lunch yesterday—very pleasant—and we also had Leslie Howard, who is going to play opposite Tallulah Bankhead in that show I adapted, *Her Cardboard Lover*. Did you know that Leslie was at Dulwich a year or two after our time? Leslie Howard is a stage name, so it's no good searching the school records. He is an awfully nice fellow and a very good writer on the side. He wrote some excellent short things, very funny, which he showed me one day in New York, and I was able to get Frank Crowninshield to take them for *Vanity Fair*.

Don't you think the curse of an author's life is the passion printers have for exclamation marks? They love to shove them in every second sentence. I've just been rereading *Piccadilly Jim*, the proofs of which I didn't correct, being in New York, and the book is bristling with them. Specimen sentence: "But wait a minute! I don't get this!" It gives an impression of febrile excitement which spoils the whole run of the dialogue.

Ian Hay is dramatizing *A Damsel in Distress*. Tom Miller and Basil Foster are putting it on. We have formed a syndicate—the management, Ian, and I each putting up five hundred pounds. We needed another five hundred to make up the necessary two thousand, and A. A. Milne gallantly stepped forward and said he would like to come in.

⌇∿⌇

Putting up money for a theatrical venture is not a practice to be recommended to anyone anxious to save his pennies, for it generally seems to happen that everybody else does nicely except the backers, and I worried a good deal about Milne's £500. I knew he could afford to lose his contribution to the kitty, for he was pulling in the doubloons in sackfuls from his Christopher Robin verses and the Winnie-the-Pooh books, but it is never pleasant to be instrumental in giving a friend a punch in the wallet, and it would have been embarrassing if the *Damsel* had flopped.

All, however, went well. It played for nearly a year and made a good profit. We followed it with a farce by Ian Hay and myself called *Baa, Baa, Black Sheep* (1929), which did a spotty 115 performances, and then really hit the jackpot with Ian's naval comedy, *The Middle Watch* (August 1929), which achieved 387 performances, bringing the melon to be cut by our quartet to £20,000, for those days a sum verging on the colossal. All the backers' money was returned to them, plus handsome dividends, and when our next two shows, *The Midshipmaid* (1931) and *Orders Are Orders* (1932), both by Ian Hay, played 227 and 193 performances respectively, we felt—as I suppose Cy Feuer and his partner Martin feel these days—that making money in the theater is almost too easy to be interesting.

Then the ebb tide set in. Ian lost his magic touch. His next three shows were disasters, and in 1935 we decided that the time had come to wind up the firm while we were still—if only a little—ahead of the game. Which was a pity, as Ian's next play, a dramatization of Edgar Wallace's thriller, *The Frog*, produced by another management, did 483 performances and made a packet.

From the viewpoint of management and backers, the 1920s were the golden age. One gets the impression, looking back, that stagehands cared nothing for money in those days and worked just for the fun of it. *A Damsel in Distress* had three sets, all quite elaborate, and it cost a little over $8,000 to produce. More or less the same conditions prevailed in New York. In 1919 I wrote a novel, *The Little Warrior*, in which a young man called Otis Pilkington puts up the cash for a

55

Broadway musical and is stunned when he finds that up to the day of the dress rehearsal the expenses of the production have amounted to "the appalling sum of thirty-two thousand eight hundred and fifty-nine dollars, sixty-eight cents."

With your kind indulgence I should like to quote further.

"He had had no notion that musical plays cost so much. The costumes alone had come to ten thousand six hundred and sixty-three dollars and fifty cents. Why, for ten thousand six hundred and sixty-three dollars and fifty cents you could dress the whole female population of New York State and have a bit left over for Connecticut. So thought Mr. Pilkington, as he read the bad news on the train. He only ceased to brood on the high cost of costuming when in the next line there smote his eye an item of four hundred and ninety-eight dollars for clothing. Clothing! Weren't costumes clothing? He was just raging over this, when something lower down in the column caught his eye.

"It was the words: Clothing . . . 187.45."

I can guarantee these figures as accurate, for they come from the dossier handed to me on the occasion when I subscribed $5,000 to a musical venture of the late Al Woods. (Never came to Broadway. Died on the road. Charles Ruggles was in it, and very good he was, too.) There was also a mysterious item, "Cut . . . $15," and another for "Frames . . . $94.50." "Props" occurred on the list no fewer than seventeen times. Whatever my future, at whatever poorhouse I might spend my declining years, I felt that I was supplied with enough props to last a lifetime.

But the point I am making is that, though we did not realize it, both I and Otis Pilkington were getting off lightly. Those musicals of ours today would have cost between $300,000 and $400,000, and how they get anybody to chip in under present conditions it is difficult to understand. Yet there never seems any lack of these intrepid heroes, and good luck to them, say I. They deserve it, and they will certainly need it.

P.G.W.

17 Norfolk Street
London W. 1
Jan. 11, 1929

Dear Bill,

The two shows are doing well. Both were over the £2,000 last week. *Her Cardboard Lover* hasn't dropped below £2,500 yet,

56

but I have an uneasy feeling that it is one of those plays that may go all to nothing at short notice, though Tallulah is terrific, as is Leslie Howard. It's very funny in spots and there is a lot of emotion, but the characters don't seem real to me. *Damsel in Distress* looks solid and ought to run a year.

Can you get anything to read these days? I was in the *Times* library last week and came out empty handed. There wasn't a thing I wanted. To fill in the time till Edgar Wallace writes another one, I'm rereading Lord Dunsany. (Edgar Wallace, by the way, now has a Rolls-Royce for personal use and also a separate car for each of the five members of his family, I hear. Also a day butler and a night butler, so that there is never a time when you can call at his house and not find buttling in progress. That's the way to live.)

I never get tired of Dunsany's stories. I can always let them cool off for a month or two and then come back to them. (All this will probably be wasted on you, as I don't suppose you've read him, unless you were attracted to his stories by the fact that they used to be illustrated by S. H. Sime. He has exactly the same eerie imagination as Sime. In fact, he told me once that quite a lot of his things were written from Sime's pictures. They would hand him a Sime drawing of a winter scene with a sinister-looking bird flying over it, and he would brood on it for a while and come up with "The Bird of the Difficult Eye.")

His secret sorrow is that he also writes plays and can't get them put on. I spent the afternoon with him once at his house down in Kent, and he read me three of his plays—yes, *three*—one after the other. Quite good, but much too fantastic. One of them was about an ex-officer after the war who couldn't get a job, so he hired himself out as a watchdog. He lived in a kennel, and the big scene was where he chased a cat up a tree and sat under it shouting abuse. I thought it funny myself, but I could just picture the fishy, glazed eye of a manager listening to it.

He told me a story about the Troubles in Ireland which amused me considerably. Lord Whoever-It-Was had a big house near Cork, and one day a gang of Sinn Feiners rolled up and battered down the front door with axes. Inside they found a very English butler, a sort of Beach of Blandings Castle, who eyed them austerely and said in a chilly voice, "His Lordship is not at home." They then went in and wrecked the place from basement to attic, finally setting fire to it. On leaving, they found the butler still standing statuesquely in the hall. Flames were darting about everywhere and ceilings coming down with a bang, but Fotheringay, or whatever his name was, was quite unperturbed. "Who shall I say called, sir?" he asked.

Dunsany came to lunch one day at Norfolk Street when I wasn't there, and Ethel, greeting him in the library, told him that he was my favorite author and that I was never happier than when curled up with one of his books and all that sort of thing. And then, to her horror, she saw his eye swiveling around the shelves and realized that there wasn't a single Dunsany opus there. The solution, of course, was that all his were in my room upstairs, where I keep the books I like best, but she didn't know that, so couldn't tell him, so I suppose for the rest of his life he will regard me as a fraud and a humbug. And no means of letting him know the truth, of course.

17 Norfolk Street
London W. 1
February 20, 1929

Dear Bill,

I finished *Big Money* the day before yesterday, and it is now at the typist's. What a comfort it is having a typist just around the corner to do carbons and things. When I was finishing *Sam in the Suburbs*—in Monte Carlo, of all places—I got a cable from the *Post* saying that they must have it immediately or they wouldn't be able to use it for another year, so I had to mail them my original script, the only one in existence. I was in a considerable twitter till I heard it had arrived safely, I having no confidence in the Monegasque postal system.

I had my usual trouble over *Big Money*. I went off the rails and had to rewrite practically all of it three times. I am now taking it easy for a bit, and as all my favorite English and American authors have let me down, I've fallen back on the French. I've read everything by Colette I could get hold of, including her autobiography, *Mes Apprentissages*. In re Colette, a thing I've never been able to understand is how her husband, Willy, got away with it. Did you ever hear of Willy? He must have been quite a chap. He was a hack journalist of sorts, and shortly after they were married he spotted Colette could write, so he locked her in a room and made her turn out the three *Claudine* books, which he published under his own name—*par* Willy, not a mention of her—and made a fortune out of. He would give her an occasional bit of the proceeds and expect her to be grateful for it, and he used to tell interviewers that his wife had been of considerable assistance to him in these works of his, helping him quite a little from time to time.

Right. One can faintly understand that aspect of his literary production, because she was very young and scared stiff of him, so I suppose she didn't dare to object. But why did all the other fellows whose work he published as his own put up with it? What he used to do was get a central idea for a novel and write a page or two and then send what he had done to a friend with a letter saying that he had got as far as this but what was needed now was the friend's magic touch. Could he, the friend, take the time to dash off a few thousand words in his own inimitable style, just to get the thing going?

When the script came back with the added stuff, he had it typed and sent it to another friend. "To the rescue, old man! You will see that enclosed is beginning to shape, but it needs you to add the touches. Could you take the time to dash off, etc.?" The script—plus the "touches"—would then go to a third friend, then a fourth and possibly a fifth, until eventually it was finished and another novel "*par* Willy" was in the bookshops.

How did he *do* it? It must have been hypnotism or something.

I was glad to get your long letter. Darned shame you had to alter the title of the new book. I can't see why, in these days when so many books are coming out, it matters if two titles clash. I see a man has just published a book called *Seventeen*. You'd have thought Booth Tarkington had established the sole right to that title, but I'll bet nobody notices anything.

I don't have much difficulty as a rule with titles; it's the plots that bother me. How do you get your plots? I like to think of some scene, it doesn't matter how crazy, and work backward and forward from it until eventually it becomes quite plausible and fits neatly into the story. Like in *Something New*, which started with my thinking it would be funny if somebody touched a cold tongue in the dark—ox tongue, I mean, not human tongue—and thought it was a corpse. I still don't know if you've read *Something New*, but that's what happens to Lord Emsworth's secretary Baxter about halfway through that opus, and it came out as smooth as butter after I had got the events leading up to it. The scene I worked to and fro from in *A Damsel in Distress* was the one where the girl jumps into the hero's cab. It isn't a bad way of getting going, at least for the sort of stuff I do, though of course it isn't always that it pans out. I've had one such scene tucked away in my notebook for two years, but haven't been able to do anything with it, owing to brain not being equal to task. I have a chap creeping along a narrow ledge outside a country house (why?) and scared stiff he's going to fall. Passes window, sees fellow inside. Raps on glass, to be let in, and fellow just gives him a nasty look and walks out of room (again why?), leaving him stranded. Absolutely nothing stirring in the way of inspiration so far, but it may click ten years from now.

❧

Actually it was a good deal longer than that before it clicked. The scene occurs in the Blandings Castle novel *Full Moon*, published in 1947.

W.T.

17 Norfolk St.
London W. 1
April 13, 1929

Dear Bill,

I think I see what's wrong with that story you sent me. You've got a star character—Captain Shuffley—and you don't give him enough to do. He just sits in the background till Page 52, and even then he doesn't do anything *ingenious*. He just produces fifty pounds and hands it over to Brogan. You might just as well not have him in the story at all, except as a mechanism for Brogan getting the money. I'm sure that's why you feel the thing is dull. You engage Charles Laughton to play a star part, and all the time the audience is saying, "Hey! Isn't Laughton going to do *anything?*"

The conception of the story is good. What it needs is for Shuffley to do something funny and ingenious in order to get the money for Brogan; he can't simply say, "I've got fifty quid. Here you are." I can't think of anything on the spur of the moment, but the sort of thing you need is something like they had in a play called *Turn to the Right*, done on Broadway around about 1916, where the comic crook learns from the old woman who has been kind to him that the local banker is going to sell her up unless she pays five hundred dollars for back rent or something. The banker comes in, the crook picks his pocket of a wad of money, and then when the banker starts demanding the five hundred from the old woman, he steps forward, produces the wad, and says, "Here you are, paid in full; gimme a receipt."

See what I mean? It showed the lead character *doing* something. You got the thing absolutely right in "Captain Shuffley's Briar Pipe," which *Collier's* bought. In this one the situation is very much the same, and Shuffley ought somehow to fool the villain and get the money from him by a trick and then hand it over to Brogan. I'm just thinking aloud, but if he went to Beigel and said, "Give me twenty-five pounds and I can kid Kirtle out of buying the land, and then you will be able to get it, and I know some hotel people want to build a hotel there," and then went to Kirtle and

61

told a similar tale, he could give both sums to Brogan, to make up the required fifty.

This might be all right if Kirtle and Beigel—you would call the poor devils names like that—were working secretly from each other. Suppose each had got a private tip that the hotel was to be built and neither knows the other knows it, and Shuffley demands twenty-five pounds from each as his price for not telling the other. If you handled it that way, you would have to conceal from the reader that he was fooling them *both*. You would have to show him telling Kirtle that he knew what he was up to and that twenty-five quid would keep him, Shuffley, quiet, and then in the end you would reveal that he had played the same game on Beigel. In fact, the more people you had working against each other, the easier it would be, because you could make Shuffley's silence money smaller. How would it be to have him get five pounds from three people—or even two, and then run it up to the required sum by gambling?

I think this might work. It has the merit of making Shuffley seem crooked till right at the end, when you reveal how pure his motives were.

17 Norfolk St.
London W. 1
May 11, 1929

Dear Bill,

This has been a big week for celebrities. I haven't been able to move a step without bumping into one. First Lord Oxford (used to be Asquith, Prime Minister, till he started going around under an alias), then Bernard Shaw, then H. G. Wells, and finally Kipling.

Asquith was fine, just one of the boys, and so were Wells and Kipling, but anyone who likes can have B. Shaw, as far as I'm concerned. I hold this truth to be self-evident, that all men are created equal, but Shaw doesn't feel that way. Too damned pleased with himself, is my verdict.

We met at lunch at Lord Astor's, and some woman who was there frisked up to him and said she was so interested about the trip to the Far East he was going to make, and so were all her family. "My daughter talks of nothing else," she said. He gave her a supercilious look. "The whole *world* is talking about my trip to the Far East," he said coldly.

Wells is quite different. He gives you the impression of having no conceit at all. He has no illusions about his works being immortal or his vogue lasting for the rest of his life. "It takes them five years to get on to you," he said when we were discussing the writing game, as if happy to feel that he had got that much time at least before he faded out. He told me he considered himself more a journalist than a novelist, and I could see what he meant. He is bubbling over with ideas and he just pours them out, not bothering about character delineation and all the rest of it. He doesn't think much of those early things of his, like *The War of the Worlds* and the short stories—or he said he didn't—but he must know how good *Kipps* and *Mr. Polly* were.

What do you think happened when we met? We shook hands, and his first remark, apropos of nothing, was "My father was a professional cricketer." A conversation stopper, if ever there was one. What a weird country England is, with its class distinctions and that ingrained snobbery you can't seem to escape from. I suppose I notice it more because I've spent so much of my time in America. Can you imagine an American, who had achieved the position Wells has, worrying because he started out in life on the wrong side of the tracks? But nothing will ever make Wells forget that his father was a professional cricketer and his mother the housekeeper at Up Park.

It was a great moment for me, meeting Kipling, though I suppose a statement like that would make the nibs purse their lips and raise their eyebrows. It's odd, this latter-day hostility to him. How the intelligentsia do seem to loathe the poor blighter, and how we of the canaille revel in his stuff. I felt like a novice being introduced to the heavyweight champ. But he was geniality itself and didn't pull rank on me. He treated me quite as an equal. "How do you end your stories, Wodehouse? I never can think how to finish mine," he said, seeming to suggest that I might give him a tip or two which would come in useful next time he took pen in hand. We had quite a long talk, and I wish I had had the nerve to ask him for an explanation of "Mrs. Bathurst," a story over which I have been brooding since boyhood.

Do you remember "Mrs. Bathurst"? I read it for the first time years ago and didn't understand a word of it. Since then I have read it half a dozen times, and it still baffles me. What did Vickery tell the Captain in his cabin that made the Captain look very grave and send him up-country, where he was struck by lightning? Who was the other fellow who was struck by lightning, too, and why was he introduced? Can anyone explain why Vickery, having seen Mrs. B. walking toward the camera in a motion picture at an English railroad station, shown at a circus in Durban, should have expressed such consternation? True, he had thought of her as still living in New Zealand, but why, even supposing that they had had a love affair, should her arrival in England when he was in South Africa have disturbed him so much? Why, too, did he make that cryptic remark to Pyecroft that his wife had died in childbirth?

Somebody—I forget who—once told me that the other fellow who was struck by lightning *was* Mrs. Bathurst. Golly!

❦

I was not alone in my imperfect sympathy with Bernard Shaw. Many others on meeting him formed the opinion that he was not their dream man. When he resigned from the Dramatists Club, the comment of Sir Arthur Wing Pinero, its president, that "Mr. Shaw's resignation is as nothing compared with ours" was received with loud applause. Arnold Bennett in his diaries gives the impression that he did not care for him much, and he cannot have endeared himself very greatly to Joseph Conrad when he opened a conversation with him by saying, "You know, your stuff really won't do, my dear fellow."

Another non-admirer was George Horace Lorimer. John Tebbel in his biography of Lorimer tells of their first and only encounter, at a luncheon given, like the one where I met him, by Lord Astor.

"They [Lorimer and Garet Garrett, one of his editors] arrived at the Astor town house and strolled into the drawing room and stood before the warmth of the fireplace. Shaw came in abruptly, saw them there, and remarked in his customary manner, 'Well, I see you Americans have all the money to travel with, as usual.' Lorimer said nothing, and Lady Astor came in, sensed the tension and hurried everyone to lunch.

"The meal was a hostess's dream of hell. Lorimer and Garrett were obviously at swords' points with Shaw. Lady Astor rushed into the silence with a choice of subject that, had she known it, could hardly have been less tactful.

" 'Mr. Shaw has written a new piece, Mr. Lorimer,' she said, 'and it's really priceless. I think you should have it for your magazine before any other American periodical gets it. Tell us about it, won't you, Mr. Shaw?'

"Mr. Shaw readily told about it, at length. When he had finished, he said, 'Of course the American magazines are all after it. Hearst has offered me a very fancy price.' He went on to describe with enjoyment the competitive bidding of American publishers for his work.

" 'I see you're on the auction block,' Lorimer said in a tone so final that it closed the subject at once."

I had been prejudiced against Shaw, even before we met, by a story Guy Bolton told me about him. Guy was making a play out of one of W. J. Locke's novels—not *The Beloved Vagabond* or *The Morals of Marcus Ordeyne;* one of the others—and he was spending a week or two at Locke's house, working with him. One day Shaw blew in, chuckling heartily. It appeared that there was a man they both knew, who lived with his sister. The man was blind, and the sister used to read aloud to him. A few days previously she had come in and found him in his usual chair and had picked up the book she was reading to him and had gone on with it. After she had been reading for twenty minutes or so, she thought it odd that he didn't make a comment of any kind, and she looked more closely and found that he was dead. Shaw roared with laughter as he told the story. "You mean you think that *funny?*" cried Locke, outraged. "Well, don't you?" said Shaw. "Sitting there reading to him for half an hour, when he was dead all the time."

Guy, who is always charitable, thinks Shaw was trying to pull Locke's leg, Locke being a sentimentalist, but I don't agree with him. I think it was just the sort of episode which he would consider hilarious.

P.G.W.

17 Norfolk Street
London W. 1
June 1, 1929

Dear Bill,

I finished *Comox* last night, and I see exactly what you mean. It's a hybrid. It starts off as a leisurely, Arnold Bennett sort of novel and then turns into a story of action, and the effect of this is to make the last part seem all out of key. It seems to me that you will have to abandon the leisurely stuff and go for action.

In writing a novel, I always imagine I'm writing for a cast of actors. (I believe I told you this before.) Some actors are natural minor actors and some are natural major ones. It's a matter of personality. Same in a book. Psmith, for instance, is a major character. If I'm going to have Psmith in a story, he must be in the big situations.

Right ho, then. In this book of yours Sennen stands out as a major character. What is the main thread of the story? Andrew's married life. Therefore, Sennen must affect that. But he doesn't. Comox does, and Comox is essentially a minor character. (And if you say he isn't, I come back at you—quick as a flash—by saying that in that case you can't drop him casually into the story on Page 200. He must run right through.) I believe the solution is to give Comox's stuff to Sennen. The main thing is, *pull the story together*. The material is all there, but the construction is wrong.

One big character is worth two small ones. Don't diffuse the interest. Generally, the trouble is that you can't switch Character A's stuff so that it fits Character B; but here Comox can blend into Sennen without a hitch.

The absolute cast-iron rule, I'm sure, in writing a story is to introduce *all* your characters as early as possible. In *Leave It to Psmith* I got the whole cast—except Ed Cootes—into the first chapter. (And a hell of a sweat it was, taxing my frail strength to the utmost.)

I think the success of every novel—if it's a novel of action—depends on the high spots. The thing to do is to say to yourself

"Which are my big scenes?" and then get every drop of juice out of them. You're a bit apt to give the same value to a minor scene as to a major. (By the way, in passing, I'm planning out a story where there are two brothers, the elder a mining engineer, the younger a major in the army. So the major is a miner and the minor a major. This causes confusion.)

It will probably be agony to rewrite this *Comox* thing—if you take my advice and do—but, boy, you don't know what trouble is. Two weeks ago I got a cable from Reynolds about my *Big Money* saying:

> *Saturday Evening Post* will buy provided you make certain changes. They like story, but think at present it is difficult to follow week by week. They suggest you might want to eliminate a character or two.

Well, you can imagine what it's like, taking even one character out of my sort of story, where a character is put in only because he's needed for a couple of big scenes later on in the book. However, I cabled that I would do it, and for the last three weeks I've been working at it like a beaver. I found that I could simplify the story enormously by dropping the whole of one motive and the characters it involved, but this meant rewriting the whole book. Whenever I came to a spot where I had been hoping to be able just to rip a dozen pages out of the original version and pin them together, I found they were studded with allusions to the vanished characters.

Your troubles may be pretty bad, but they were part of the first draft, when one expects to encounter a snag or two, but from the tone of Reynolds' cable I gather that my brainchild practically got over as it stood, and then some ass in the office said, "Of course, Mr. Lorimer, it wouldn't be a bad thing if there were fewer characters," and George Horace Lorimer yawned and said, "Something in that, kid. Tell him to cut out a couple of them."

I'm very interested in what you say about Freddie Rooke in *The Little Warrior*. Too much the conventional stage dude, as Bertie Wooster was when I started writing him. If you look at the early Jeeves stories, you'll find Bertie quite a different character now.

17 Norfolk Street
London W. 1
September 3, 1929

Dear Bill,

Sorry not to have written before, but I have been tied up with a very difficult story (short). "Company for Gertrude" I'm calling it. It's one of those maddening yarns where you get the beginning and end all right and can't think what to put in the middle. It's a Lord Emsworth story, and the idea is that he has been landed with a niece at the castle, said niece having got engaged to a man her family disapproves of, a pal of Freddie Threepwood's. She has been sent to Blandings to get her out of the man's way. Freddie remembers having seen a film where the same thing happened and the humble suitor, disguised with false whiskers, oiled into the house and sucked up to the family, and then, when they were all crazy about him, tore off his whiskers and asked for their blessing. So he sends the hero to stay at Blandings, telling Lord E. he is a friend of his named Popjoy. He tells hero to strain every nerve to ingratiate himself with Lord E.

Now, you see what happens. The fellow spends his whole time hanging around Lord Emsworth, helping him out of chairs, asking him questions about the gardens and so on, and it simply maddens Lord E., who feels he has never loathed a young man more. Well, what is bothering me is the getting of the cumulative details which lead up to Lord E. loathing the young man. Can you think of any? What *would* a fellow in that position do, thinking he was making a hit with the old man when really he was driving him off his head?

I suspended work on my novel temporarily, in order to write this story, when I was halfway through it. I always think it's a good thing to put a long story aside and tackle something else be-

68

fore you go stale on it. It has come out well so far. To refresh your memory, the novel is *Hot Water*, which I told you about some time ago when I was scenarioing it out. The aunt has been eliminated altogether, as has the hero's father. I scrapped four versions of the first 30,000 words. My main trouble is that my heroine refuses to come alive, and what makes it worse is that the second girl is a pippin. I'm afraid the reader will skip all the hero and heroine parts and concentrate on the scenes between the second man and the second girl.

What a sweat a novel is when you aren't sure of your characters. And what a vital thing it is to give the major characters plenty to do. That is the test. If they aren't in situations, characters can't be major characters, not even if you have the rest of the troop talk their heads off about them.

Cheering news from India. My press clipping agency has sent me a letter from the correspondence column of an Indian paper about a cow that came into the bungalow of a Mr. Verrier Elwyn, who lives at Patengarth, Mandla District, and ate his copy of *Carry On, Jeeves*, "selecting it from a shelf which contained, among other works, books by Shakespeare, Thomas Hardy and Henry Fielding." A pretty striking tribute I look on that as.

The day before yesterday I was rung up and told that Flo Ziegfeld wanted to speak to me from New York. After a lot of waiting I was told that the phone call had been canceled. He cabled instead. He wants me to go over there immediately to help with a musical comedy. He said he was arranging for my passage through an agency who would communicate with me, so I suppose this means sailing next Wednesday. Ethel won't be coming with me this time, as I don't expect to stay in America more than a few weeks. Agony being parted from her, but I'm glad to be going, as I shall be able to see my adaptation of *Candlelight*, which Gertrude Lawrence is starring in. Gilbert Miller is putting it on.

Dear Bill,

I am having the usual Ziegfeld experience. I've been here six weeks, and nothing has happened yet.

The show he wanted me for is a musical version of a play called *East Is West*, a very big success as a straight play in 1918. It's all about a Chinese girl who goes around saying "Me love Chlistian god velly much" and all that sort of prune juice, and turns out in the end to be the daughter of an American missionary, kidnaped by the Chinese in her infancy. I think it's frightful, but I suppose Flo is fascinated by the thought of how he will be able to spread himself over the costumes, and anyway I haven't anything to do with the writing of the book, just the lyrics. Bill McGuire is doing the book; at least, he's supposed to be, but as far as I can make out he hasn't started yet. He always was a leisurely sort of bird.

The music is by Vincent Youmans, if he ever gets around to doing any, and I am collaborating on the lyrics with a fellow called Billy Rose, a very nice chap and very much of a live wire. He's one of those lads who always give me the feeling that they're living about six times as fast as I am and are equal to anything. Apart from being, I believe, the fastest shorthand writer in America, he has run successful nightclubs, the sort of places where the Purple Mob from Detroit come in with tommy guns and start off by ordering a thousand dollars' worth of champagne. And with all that a very good lyrist, too. As far as I can make out, he and I are the only members of the gang who are doing a stroke of work. I go around to his hotel every morning and we hammer out a lyric together and turn it in to Youmans, after which nothing more is heard of it.

So what with this and what with that it seemed to me a good idea to take a few days off and go to Hollywood. I wanted to see what the place was like before committing myself to it for an extended period. I was there three days, but, having in an absent-minded moment forgotten to tell Flo and Gilbert Miller that this was only a flying visit and that when the fields were white with daisies I would return, I created something of an upheaval in the bosoms of both. Flo wanted to have me around, as he expected Bill McGuire and Youmans to come out of their respective trances at any moment, and rehearsals of *Candlelight*, the thing Gertrude Lawrence is starring in, were nearing their end and the out-of-town opening coming along, so Gilbert Miller wanted me around, too. It was a nasty jar, therefore, when they were told that I had gone to Hollywood, presumably for good.

It hit Flo hardest, because he loves sending 1,000-word telegrams telling people what he thinks of them, and he had no address where he could reach me. From what Billie Burke (Mrs. Flo) told me later, I gather that he nearly had apoplexy. However, all was forgotten and forgiven when I returned on the ninth day. I went to Baltimore, where *Candlelight* was playing, and got rather a chilly reception from Gertie, but was eventually taken back into the fold.

Candlelight has since opened in New York and looks like a hit. Gertie is wonderful, as always. This is the first time she has done a nonmusical show, but she is just as good as she was in *Oh, Kay!* I don't believe there's anybody on the stage who can do comedy better.

The only person I knew at all well in Hollywood was Marion Davies, who was in *Oh Boy*, the show Guy Bolton, Jerry Kern, and I did for the Princess Theatre. She took me out to her house in Santa Monica and worked me into a big lunch that M-G-M were giving for Winston Churchill. All very pleasant, but I have reluctantly come to the conclusion that I must have one of those meaningless faces which make no impression whatever on the beholder. This was—I think—the seventh time I had been introduced to Churchill, and I could see that I came upon him as a complete surprise once more. Not a trace of the Addison Simms of Seattle stuff. Do you remember those advertisements of a memory course which used to appear in all the American magazines? They showed the man who had not taken the course embarrassed and floundering when he met the old acquaintance whose name he had forgotten; but the man who had taken the course just stretched out his hand with a beaming smile and said: "Why, certainly I remember you, Mr. Addison Simms. We met at the Rotary Club in Seattle on the night of October the third, 1910. How are you, Addison, old man? How are Mrs. Simms and the three children? And how did you come out on that granary deal?"

I expect to be back in England early in November, in time to see some of the Dulwich games. We seem to have a great team this year, and I'm hoping we beat Haileybury, which we ought to do after that victory over Bedford. It's rather funny how we regard the Bedford match. Nobody who has written to me seems at all pleased at having beaten them by twenty-five points. They seem to take it for granted that Bedford for once must have had a very bad team, and not that we have a good one. They appear to think there's something rather indecent about beating Bedford by twenty-five points.

17 Norfolk Street
London W. 1
November 21, 1929

Dear Bill,

No, that Stock Exchange crash didn't wipe me out, thank goodness, because I had bought all my stocks outright and not on margin. But it knocked my capital for a loop, blast it, and, like a good many other people, I'm wishing it hadn't happened. I believe Jerry Kern got very badly hit. Let's not talk about it.

I'm longing to get down and see you, but I'm in the middle of a story, which I must finish before I can make a move. I've gone and let myself in for one of those stories which work up to a big comic scene and now I'm faced with writing the scene and it looks as if it was going to be difficult to make funny. It's a village Rugger match, where everybody is trying to slay everybody else, described by Bertie Wooster, who, of course, knows nothing about

Rugby football. It's pretty hard to describe a game you know backward through the eyes of somebody who doesn't understand it. I'm calling it "The Ordeal of Young Tuppy" (Tuppy Glossop being one of the players), and I suppose it will work out all right in the end. These things generally do. But it isn't easy.

I've just heard from the agent I got in touch with when I went to Hollywood that Metro-Goldwyn-Mayer want to sign me up—six months at $2,500 a week with an option for another six months. I've cabled him to grab the offer. I shall be going out there at the end of May.

Metro-Goldwyn-Mayer
Culver City, Cal.
June 26, 1930

Dear Bill,

Well, yes and no in answer to your question Do I like Hollywood? I like the place and the weather and particularly the people. About everybody I know in the Broadway theater is here, plus a large contingent from London, so one has lots of congenial society. Interesting conversationalists in every nook and cranny.

When the Talkies came in and they had to have dialogue, the studios started handing out contracts right and left to everyone who had ever written a line of it. Only an author of exceptional ability and determination could avoid getting signed up. And if you didn't want to be a writer, they would be just as pleased to take you on as a diction teacher or a voice specialist. With the result that the migration to Hollywood has been like one of those great race movements of the Middle Ages. So though there is a touch of desert island about the place and one feels millions of miles from anywhere, one can always count on meeting half a dozen kindred spirits when one is asked out to dinner.

It's the work I don't like, if you can call it work. They have this extraordinary idea that if one writer can do a good job, ten will do ten times as good a one. They believe in everybody getting into the act. The first assignment they gave me was a picture called *Three French Girls*, and they handed me a script complete to the last fade-out, the work, I suppose, of about twenty scriveners. If it had been just a scenario, I would have been able to do something with it, but it was a finished production all ready for shooting, situations excellent, dialogue fine, nothing needing altering in it as far as I could see. I wrote in a couple of gag lines, and then I had shot my bolt. After that I heard nothing of it and nothing from the studio. I had told them I wanted to work at home, and the arrangement was that if I was needed, they would phone me. It is now four weeks since I heard from them, so I have drawn $10,000 for swimming in our pool and getting ahead with my novel *Hot Water*. Fine from one point of view, but not so good if you have a conscience and don't like taking money under false pretenses.

How is everything your end? Are you selling your stuff all right? By the way, I hope you took the advice I gave you once about not tearing up unsatisfactory stories. You never know when you will need them. I wrote a Ukridge story last year which seemed to me no good, and if I hadn't made this rule about always keeping what I write, I should have destroyed it. Last week I suddenly realized that it wasn't a Ukridge story at all but a Bingo Little one, and I did it all over again from that angle and the result is fine. I haven't actually sent it out yet, but I know the *Post* will take it. Quite a few bits from the first version appear in the second, and if I had wastepaper-basketed it a year ago, I should never have been able to remember them.

I heartily concur, as they say, with your criticism of "Reggie and the Greasy Bird." In the shape in which you saw it, rotten. It just shows how much depends on the telling of a story. It may be all right except for one little thing which put the editor off without his knowing why he was put off. That was one of the ways I went off the rails in the Ukridge story. I had a scene where Ukridge gets in bad with the man who was going to give him a job, and it didn't seem right. Even when I changed it to a Bingo Little story, it still seemed wrong, and finally I spotted that what was killing the whole yarn was this one scene. I had Ukridge meeting the prospective employer at Charing Cross Station, and while they were talking along came one of U's creditors and U breaks off in the middle of a sentence and legs it, thus making the prospective employer feel that he is a bit too eccentric to have on his payroll.

Why that wasn't right, I'm still darned if I know. It sounds a good enough scene. But it was all wrong, and I substituted a quite short and simple conversation at the employer's club. I think the trouble may have been that it was too big a scene for that point in the story. In other words, I had put an Act Two scene into Act One.

Metro-Goldwyn-Mayer Studio
Culver City, Cal.
August 18, 1930

Dear Bill,

Your letter just arrived. That's fine about the story you sold to the *Post*.

Ethel arrived a month ago, with Susan's daughter Winks under her arm. Winks has settled down finally and seems to be happy, but it must be a testing experience for a dog of regular habits suddenly to be jerked out of her home and taken to California.

I expect to be out here till next spring. I might dash back to England for a week or two before that, but I'm not counting on it, as I expect they will want me to stick on without going away.

We have a delightful house—Norma Shearer's—with a small but lovely garden and a big swimming pool. I spend most of my time in the pool.

Odd place, this. On the surface everything seems peaceful and jolly, everybody all smiles and hands slapping backs on every side, but it doesn't take you long after you've settled down here and talked to a few usually well-informed sources to realize that conditions are rather like what they must be among the gangsters in Chicago, plots and counterplots and struggles for power and all that sort of thing. Irving Thalberg, for instance, the man I'm working for, is in a constant state of war with Louis B. Mayer, the big chief of the studio, though nobody would guess it to hear them cooing at each other on the telephone.

The trouble is that when Thalberg came to M-G-M at the age of nineteen or so, Mayer looked on him simply as a promising young fellow on whom he would keep a fatherly eye and hadn't a notion that there was ever going to be anything in the nature of competition between them. And then after a few years Thalberg suddenly became the big noise in the firm, with everybody talking of him as the genius of M-G-M and the man who got things done, which of course was agony for Mayer. He felt the lad had done him wrong and betrayed his trust in him, the rule here being the same as the one that prevails in barbershops—viz., "You must shave well, but you mustn't shave better than the boss."

Still, he might have been able to keep a stiff upper lip if it had been just a matter of applause and bouquets, but Thalberg kept demanding more and more money, which cut him to the quick. Everyone seems to think things are working up to explosion point. Not that it matters much to humble hirelings like me, of course, but there must be scores of directors, supervisors, and whatnot who are all of a twitter, wondering what the harvest will be. Because in these studio civil wars the side that loses gets massacred in droves.

If the palace revolution does break out, you will find me rooting for Thalberg. As nice a chap as I've met for a long time, sensitive, artistic, and courteous, his only fault being a tendency to tell you to come and see him at four sharp, not a minute later, and keep you waiting in the anteroom till seven-thirty. And even that has its compensations, for you find the anteroom full of the fellows he told to see him at two sharp and three sharp, and they are always interesting to talk to. I've got an idea for a short story where a gorilla, featured in the big celluloid epic *Darkest Africa*, escapes from its cage on the M-G-M lot and everybody is in a panic because it may look in on Thalberg, who is known to be working in his office, and do him a bit of no good. Then somebody remembers that it can't possibly get into Thalberg's office without waiting four hours in the anteroom, and they all calm down.

Meanwhile, I am still a gentleman of leisure or, you might say, more like a remittance man getting his weekly dole. There was talk the other day of my making a picture out of *Candlelight* for John Gilbert, but nothing has come of it yet, and I don't see how the play can be twisted to make it a vehicle for a male star. I don't know if you saw it when it was running in London (Harry Graham's version), but it has two equal male roles, the Prince and his valet, which Reggie Owen and Leslie Howard are playing over here, and you couldn't make one of them a star part without upsetting the whole balance of the thing, especially as the Gertie Lawrence part is just as good as the two men's. If they do it at all, it ought to be done with three stars of equal importance. But, ask me, I think the whole thing will blow over. Unless there's what Conan Doyle would call villainy afoot.

For a disturbing thought has occurred to me. When John Gilbert did his first talkie, his voice was hopeless. It came out all shrill and squeaky and his popularity with the fans died overnight, rendering him a total loss to the studio. Well, disasters like that are happening all the time these days—I mean big silent stars turning out to be no good when they speak lines—and you might have supposed that the brass hats would just have dropped a tear and said, "Too bad, too bad; still, that's the way it goes," and turned their thoughts to other things. But here's the catch. Just before he did that first talkie they had signed him up for four more at $250,000 apiece, and the thought of having to pay out those million smackers gashes them like a knife. The rumor goes that in order to avoid this they are straining every nerve to ensure that his next picture will be such a flop that he will consent to make a brokenhearted settlement and retire from the screen. And what is disturbing me is this. Do they feel that I am the only writer on the payroll who can be relied on to deliver a flop? When it is essential that a motion picture shall lay an egg and be a hissing and a byword, does the cry go around the front office, "Wodehouse is the man! Send for Wodehouse!"

It makes you think.

Dear Bill,

M-G-M have taken up my option and I am with them for another six months. Ethel has rented this house for a year, so I suppose I shall stay here that long. I may get another contract at the end of the six months, of course, but I doubt it, as so far I have been only of ornamental value to the studio. No question that I lend the place a tone—my new sports shirts ensure this—but will M-G-M feel that it's worth paying $2,500 a week just to give the populace an eyeful? They could get someone equally dressy for half that.

On the other hand, I have made myself so pleasant to all the studio heads that by now I may count as a cousin by marriage or even a brother-in-law. Very moot, the whole thing.

Meanwhile, they've put me on to *Rosalie*, that thing which Guy Bolton, Bill McGuire, Ira Gershwin, George Gershwin, Sigmund Romberg, and I did for Ziegfeld. M-G-M bought the picture rights for Marion Davies and immediately decided, as they always do out here when they buy anything, that it would have to have a different story. All the finest minds on the lot had a shot at it, but apart from the novel idea that the heroine should be dressed as a boy, God knows why, nobody came up with anything that satisfied the front office, and while scraping the bottom of the barrel they found me. After I had messed about with the thing with my usual non-success for a while, Thalberg worked out a story on his own and summoned me to Santa Barbara, where he was spending a few days, to hear it.

I drove down there with a stenographer from the studio, and he dictated a complete scenario. When he had finished, he leaned back and mopped his brow, and asked me if I wanted to have it read over to me. I was about to say yes, just to make the party go, when I suddenly caught the stenographer's eye and was startled to see a look of agonized entreaty in it. I couldn't imagine what was wrong, but she so unmistakably wanted me to say no that I said no, and she sank back in her chair with a little moan of relief. When we were driving home, she told me she had had a latish night the night before and had dozed off at the outset of the proceedings and slept peacefully throughout, not having heard or taken down a word. And as the whole thing, except for a little bit here and a little bit there, has completely passed from my mind, I don't see how my version is going to electrify the industry. I shall be lucky if it turns out merely colossal.

I am still swimming vigorously three times a day, though in the early morning the water is pretty chilly. They tell me that if you don't mind being frozen a bit you can bathe here all through the winter.

In spite of my plaintive protests, Ethel gave a big party the other night. There was a mob milling around, polluting our nice garden, from four in the afternoon till midnight. About twenty people in the pool at one time. All the stars were there. The one advantage of having a party in your own home is that you can sneak away. I went up to my room at five and only appeared for dinner, returning to my room at eight sharp. (The perfect host, they sometimes call me.) I passed the hours rereading Maugham's *Cakes And Ale*. What a masterly book it is. Incidentally, if they were going to pick on anyone for being irreverent toward the old Victorian master, why not Hugh Walpole for his *Hans Frost?* Did you read that one?

I can't remember if you said you liked or disliked Dorothy Parker's *Laments for the Living*. I've just got it, and it's good.

We are toying with a scheme for going around the world on the "Empress of Britain" when we leave here. Sometimes we feel we should like it, and then we ask ourselves if we really want to see the ruddy world. I'm darned if I know. I've never seen any spectacular spot yet that didn't disappoint me. I've always liked wandering about in the background. I mean, I get much more kick out of a place like Droitwich, which has no real merits, than out of something like Niagara Falls or the Grand Canyon.

Dear Bill,

Since I last wrote, I have been spending a week at Hearst's ranch. He owns 400,000 acres, more than the whole of Long Island.

The ranch—ranch, my foot; it's a castle—is about halfway between Hollywood and San Francisco. It's on the top of a high hill, and just inside the entrance gates is a great pile of stones which, if you ever put them together, would form an old abbey which Hearst bought in France and shipped over and didn't know what to do with, so left lying by the wayside. The next thing you see, having driven past this, is a yak or a buffalo or some other creature of the wild in the middle of the road. Hearst collects everything, including animals, and has a zoo on the premises, and the specimens considered reasonably harmless are allowed to roam at large. You're apt to meet a bear or two before you get to the house, or an elephant, or even Sam Goldwyn.

There are always at least fifty guests staying here. All the furniture is period, mostly with the sales tags still attached, and you probably sleep in a bed originally occupied by Napoleon or somebody. Ethel and I shared the Venetian suite with Sidney Blackmer, who had blown in from one of the studios.

The train that takes guests away leaves after midnight, and the one that brings new guests arrives early in the morning, so you have dinner with one lot of people and come down to breakfast next morning and find an entirely fresh crowd. No drinks are allowed after dinner, which must come as a nasty blow to many, though perhaps they might have refused them anyway after seeing that yak in the road. A man has to be a pretty tough toper not to knock off after the shock of finding yaks among those present.

Meals take place in an enormous room hung with banners, and are served at a long table, with Hearst sitting in the middle on one side and Marion Davies in the middle on the other. The longer you're there, the further you get from the middle. I sat on Marion's right the first night, then found myself getting edged further and further away, till I got to the extreme end, when I thought it time to leave. Another day and I should have been feeding on the floor.

You don't see Hearst till dinnertime, and then, if you're a sensitive soul like me and sitting immediately opposite him, you might wish you hadn't seen him then. In my experience there are two kinds of elderly American. One, the stout and horn-rimmed, is mateyness itself. He greets you as if you were a favorite son, starts agitating the cocktail shaker before you know where you are, slips a couple into you with a merry laugh, tells you a dialect story about two Irishmen named Pat and Mike, and in a word makes life one grand sweet song. The other, which runs a good deal to the tight lips and the cold gray stare, seems to view the English cousin with concern. It is not elfin. It broods. It says little. And every now and then you catch its eye, and it is like colliding with a raw oyster.

Mine host belongs to the latter class. He's a sinister old devil, not at all the sort I'd care to meet down a lonely alley on a dark night. Looks to me always as if he was plotting something, probably a murder.

10 Benedict Canyon Drive
Beverly Hills, Cal.
March 14, 1931

Dear Bill,

This business of writing letters abroad has taken on a graver aspect, the postal authorities here having raised the ante to five cents a throw. I can bear it bravely as far as you are concerned, but I do grudge having to spend five cents answering a letter from some female in Lesser-Snodsbury-in-the-Vale who wants to know if I pronounce my name Woodhouse or Woadhouse.

My art is not going well at the moment. Some time ago the *American* Magazine commissioned six short stories from me at, if you can believe it, $6,000 per for American first serial rights—and I shall be getting £500 per from the *Strand* for the English first serial rights in addition to that. Must be a record—and ye Ed has put me right out of my stride by telling me, after seeing the first two, that he wants the others to be about American characters in an American setting, little knowing that if I try to do American stuff, the result is awful. Apparently he doesn't care for Mulliner stories, though I'll swear things like "Anselm Gets His Chance" and "The Fiery Wooing of Mordred" aren't bad, always provided you like my sort of stuff. What puzzles me about it all is that when he commissioned the series he must have known the kind of thing I write. It can't have come on him as a stunning shock to find that I was laying my scene in England. What did he expect from me? Thoughtful studies of sharecropper life in the Deep South?

I suppose I could have taken a strong line and refused haughtily to change my act, but I'm all for strewing a little happiness as I go by, so I told him I would have a pop at some Hollywood stories. I've done rather a good one about a Nodder, which is something like a Yes-man, only lower in the social scale. A Yes-man's duty is to attend studio conferences and say yes. A Nodder's is to nod. The boss throws out some statement of opinion and looks about him expectantly. This is the cue for the senior Yes-man to say yes. He is followed, in order of precedence, by the second Yes-man—or Vice-Yesser, as he is sometimes called—and the junior Yes-men. Only when all the Yes-men have yessed do the Nodders begin to function. They nod. It's not a very exalted position, lying somewhere between that of the man who works the wind machine and that of a writer of additional dialogue. There is also a class of Untouchables known as Nodders' Assistants, but this is a technicality with which I need not trouble you. The hero of my story is a full Nodder.

Dear Bill,

As I expected, M-G-M have not taken me on for another year. I don't blame them. After all, I've done practically nothing since I got here except write a novel and six short stories, get an attractive suntan, and perfect my Australian crawl in the swimming pool. I'm no good to these people. Lay off old Pop Wodehouse is the advice I would give to any studio that wants to get on in the world. There is no surer road to success.

I doubt, though, if many writers are getting fat contracts these days. We seem to be having a sort of second installment of the 1929 depression, and the movies are taking it on the chin in a big way. Story going the rounds illustrating this. Man standing in the crowd outside a picture house after an opening hears the carriage starter calling for "Mr. Warner's automobile," "Mr. Lasky's automobile," "Mr. Louis B. Mayer's automobile," etc., and shakes his head. "At an opening a year from now," he says, "there won't be any of this stuff about automobiles. You'll hear them calling for Mr. Warner's bicycle, Mr. Lasky's kiddie car, and Mr. Louis B. Mayer's roller skates."

Did you hear anything from Doubleday? I wrote to him, urging him to publish your books in America, but have heard nothing, except that Watt told me Doubleday had told him he had had "a very nice letter" from me. Meanwhile, a writer here named John Farrow was saying the other day how much he liked your work, especially *Tiger Bay*. He is a man who served before the mast at one time, and he said how well you know the sea and wanted to know if you had ever been a sailor.

Just been reading J. B. Priestley's *Angel Pavement*. Very good, I thought, but what a curious method of writing he has. A lot of characters with practically no connection with each other are attended to in turn. For instance, you get fifty pages of Smeeth at home, then fifty pages of Dursingham at home—in separate compartments, you might say. I always feel I have to link my characters up. I mean, if I showed Smeeth at home, I would have to bring on Dursingham somehow, to play a scene with him. I suppose both methods are OK and it's just a matter of how you happen to feel about construction.

Heard a good story the other day. Wilton Lackaye, the actor, was playing in San Francisco, and he invited the editor of one of the San Francisco papers to dinner. The editor said he was sorry but he couldn't come, as he would be tied up in a conference. "A conference?" said Lackaye. "What's that for?" The editor explained. "We get together every day for an hour or so and decide what is to be in the next day's paper—matters of policy, emphasis on news, and all that sort of thing." "Good heavens!" said Lackaye, amazed. "Do you mean to tell me that you get out that paper *deliberately?*"

Listen. If you want to make a pot of money, come over here and go into domestic service. A man and his wife came from England some years ago and got a job as butler and cook at $200 a month plus their board and lodging. They were able to salt away $150 bucks each pay day. After they had been in this place for a while, they accepted an offer from a wealthier family at $300. They had two rooms and bath and everything they wanted in the way of food and wines and were able to put away $250 a month.

About a year later their employer made the mistake of entertaining a Hollywood producer for the weekend, and the producer was so struck by the couple's virtuosity that he lured them away with an offer of $400, plus all expenses, including a car. They now banked $350 a month. And when a rival producer tried to snatch them, the original producer raised their salary to $500, at which figure it remains at moment of going to press. They now own an apartment house in Los Angeles.

I heard of some people here who engaged a maid who had just come over from Finland. She seemed a nice girl and willing, but it turned out there were chinks in her armor. "How is your cooking?" they asked. She said she couldn't cook. At home her mother had always done all the cooking. "How about housework?" No, she couldn't do housework—back in Finland her aunt had always attended to all that sort of thing—nor could she look after children, her eldest sister's specialty. "Well, what *can* you do?" they asked. She thought a moment. "I can milk reindeer," she said.

So if you can milk reindeer, come along. Wealth and fame await you.

Domaine de la Fréyère
Auribeau
Alpes-Maritimes, France
March 6, 1932

Dear Bill,

The above is now my address. We have taken this place for a year. It is a Provençal country house with a hundred acres of hillside and large grounds and a huge swimming pool, belonging to some people called Orr-Lewis. It ought to be lovely in summer. Just at the moment it is a bit bleak. We are on a plateau up in the mountains about twelve miles from Cannes, with wonderful views.

I have written one goodish story since I got here, a Mulliner story called *Strychnine in the Soup*, and two others which aren't right. I think I can fix them, but a comic story that goes off the rails is worse than any other kind. One gets the feeling that one's stuff isn't funny, which is deadly.

I bought Aldous Huxley's *Brave New World* thing but couldn't get through it. What a bore these stories of the future are. The whole point of Huxley is that he can write about modern life better than anybody else, so of course he goes and writes about the future, blast him. Michael Arlen is down here. I ran into him in Cannes the other day and asked him what he was working on. "A novel," he said. "Like *The Green Hat?*" I said. "Oh, no," he said; "it's a story about the future."

I am working away at *Thank You, Jeeves*. The stuff you sent me about the house with the mice in it was just what I needed. It fits in perfectly. The setup is that Bertie Wooster's pal Chuffy lives at Chuffnell Hall down in Somersetshire, Chuffy's aunt and her son at the dower house in the park. The son breeds white mice. They smell, and the aunt thinks it's drains, so she and son shift to the Hall, leaving dower house empty. So when Bertie breaks in to get a night's lodging with his face covered with black shoe polish . . . golly, what rot it sounds when one writes it down! Come, come, Wodehouse, is *this* the best you can do in the way of carrying on the great tradition of English Literature?

Still, it really does work out all right, and I'll bet the plot of *Hamlet* sounded just as crazy when Shakespeare tried to tell it to Ben Jonson at the Mermaid Tavern. ("Well, Ben, look, it's like this: the lead character is this guy who's in love with the girl, but her old man doesn't think he's leveling with her, so he tells her . . . no, wait a minute, I better start at the beginning. Well, so this guy's in college, see, and he's come home on account his mother's married his uncle, see, and there's a ghost horsing around and he runs into this ghost and it turns out it's his father and it tells him to drop everything and murder his uncle, on account it was him that murdered him, if you see what I mean. So one thing leads to another and the guy murders the girl's old man . . .")

I haven't read *Magnolia Street*, so I don't know how good it is, but if it's as long as you say, I have my doubts. I think most novels would be better if shorter.

In re short story series. My own experience is that, unless you're extraordinarily inventive, you can't write a series bang off. I started writing in 1902, and every day, knowing that that was the thing to do, if you wanted to get on, I said to myself, "I must get a character for a series." In 1916 I wrote the first Jeeves story. A year later I wrote another one. But it wasn't till I had done about twenty at long intervals that I realized I had a series character, and by that time I had decided to give up short Jeeves stories and write Jeeves novels. That's Life.

Domaine de la Fréyère
Auribeau, A.-M.
August 13, 1932

Dear Bill,

How's everything going with you? I liked your "Before and After" story in *Collier's*.

Would this idea be any good to you? Downtrodden young man, much snootered by aunts, etc., has become engaged to two girls at once, both horrible, and feels that the only way out is to vanish. He runs away to sea on one of your tramp ships and has adventures. I admit that's not giving you much to go on, but it might work out into something.

I'm hoping that this rise in the American stock market means the beginning of better times out there. There's no doubt that the American magazines are having a bad time, and it must be difficult to land a story with them at the moment, as most of them are living on their accumulated material and are not buying anything new. Fancy the *Saturday Evening Post* people having to pass their dividend! Two years ago they were paying eight dollars a share. I don't remember if I told you, but when I sold *Thank You, Jeeves,* to the *Cosmopolitan,* they were supposed to pay me $50,-000. What they are doing is paying me in installments, so much every month. I've never heard of that happening before. Surely, even in these depression times, Hearst can't be as hard up as all that.

Odd your not getting *Louder and Funnier.* I sent it off quite a month ago. This confirms my view that only about one letter in five sent from this bally place ever arrives anywhere, and parcels haven't a hope. The postman probably drops anything at all heavy down a ravine, and I don't blame him. The poor devil has to walk miles up and down hill in the blazing sun. I'll write to the Fabers to send you a copy, but it isn't really much of a book; it's just a collection of articles I wrote for *Vanity Fair* in 1914-15-16. The best thing about it is the jacket by Rex Whistler.

Second Test Match. How about it? What a bunch of rabbits the

87

England team are. It's odd how cricketers who seem marvels during the county season are no good when they get to Australia.

Have you ever read Warwick Deeping? I hadn't till the other day when Ethel took one of his things out of the library in Cannes. He's good. His stuff reminds me a little of yours.

I have had a devil of a time with my new novel. It's a sequel to *Fish Preferred*, to be called *Heavy Weather*, and the early chapters were very hard to write, because I had to be careful not to assume that people had read *Fish Preferred* and at the same time not to put in yards of explanation which would have bored those who had. In order to get 100 pages of OK stuff, I must have written nearly 100,000 words.

This place is congested with Ethel's adopted cats, all having kittens.

Except for a tendency to write articles about the Modern Girl and allow his side-whiskers to grow, there is nothing an author has to guard himself against more carefully than the Saga habit. The least slackening of vigilance and he is hooked. He writes a story. Another story dealing with the same characters occurs to him, and he writes that. He feels that just one more won't hurt him, and he writes a third. And before he knows where he is, the thing has got him. He is down with a Saga, and no cure in sight.

This is what happened to me with Bertie Wooster and Jeeves, and again with Lord Emsworth, his son Frederick, his butler Beach, his pig the Empress, and the other residents of Blandings Castle. Beginning with *Something New*, I went on to *Leave It to Psmith*, then to *Fish Preferred*, and after that to *Heavy Weather*, *Blandings Castle*, *The Crime Wave at Blandings*, *Uncle Fred in the Springtime*, *Full Moon*, *Pigs Have Wings*, and *Service with a Smile*. And to show the habit-forming nature of the drug, while it was eight years after *Something New* before the urge of *Leave It to Psmith* gripped me, only eighteen months elapsed between *Fish Preferred* and *Heavy Weather*. In a word, once a man who could take it or leave it alone, I had become an addict.

The question of how long an author is to be allowed to go on recording the adventures of any given set of characters is one that has frequently engaged the attention of thinking men. It is more than forty years since, an eager lad in my middle thirties, I started writing Jeeves and Blandings Castle stories, and many people think this nuisance should now cease. Carpers say that enough is enough. Cavilers say the same. But against this must be set the fact that writing these stories gives me a great deal of pleasure and keeps me out of the saloons.

At what conclusion, then, do we arrive?

Very difficult to say.

So far I have written thirty-four Jeeves short stories, nine Jeeves novels, eleven Blandings Castle short stories, and ten Blandings Castle novels, and those inclined to the gloomy view no doubt feel that there is no reason why I should ever stop. They look down the vista of the years and see these chronicles multiplying like rabbits, and the prospect appalls them. But let them take heart. I shall be eighty next month, and after eighty even an author who has got the Saga habit in its most virulent form is bound to slow up. There should be, if not a complete stoppage, at any rate a lull.

P.G.W.

Domaine de la Fréyère
Auribeau, A.-M.
February 9, 1933

Dear Bill,

Sorry I haven't answered yours of January 23 before. My plans are a little uncertain. I am waiting to hear from Ethel, who left on Sunday to open the Norfolk Street house, leaving me with Winky. She is going to find out how to smuggle Winky into England and then write me. I expect a letter tomorrow. If she says come along, I shall start at once. I'm pretty sick of this place. I am all alone in the house with the caretaker and his wife, who cooks for me.

I could go and stay at a hotel in Cannes, of course, but Winky would be such a burden at a hotel. My God, she's bad enough here! She won't let me out of her sight. I need an exercise walk in the afternoon, but every time I try to start on one Winky sits on the terrace and just looks at me. You can hear her saying, "Going to leave me, eh? Well, of all the dirty tricks!" So I say,

"Well, come along too." And she says, "What, sweat down that mountain and have to sweat up again? Not for me." So it ends in my strolling about the garden.

∿

All good dog lovers chafe at the law that a dog entering England has to stay in quarantine for six months, and I am happy to say that we smuggled Winky in all right. It involved hiring an airplane with a pilot who thought on his feet (and, of course, when seated at the controls). Outwardly, despite his great brain, he was the Bertie Wooster type, the very picture of the silly ass, and this stood him in good stead in the tricky moments of the affair. Instead of stopping at Lympne, as all pilots from France have to do, he flew to his house, landed in a handy field, put Winky in storage, and flew back to Lympne full of apologies and with many an "I say, you chaps, I'm most frightfully sorry, but it absolutely slipped my mind that I was supposed to clock in here," and was properly ticked off by the authorities, who fortunately were so busy telling him what they thought of him and what would happen to him if he ever did it again that they failed to notice that he was thickly covered in Peke hairs. Winky is an affectionate dog, and she had curled up in his lap throughout the flight.

P.G.W.

Hotel Prince de Galles
Paris
June 11, 1934

Dear Bill,

Sorry I haven't answered your letter before. I've been sweating away at *The Luck of the Bodkins* and must be getting a bit stale, as I simply hadn't the energy to write a line after the day's work. It's a curious thing about this novel, and probably means that it's going to be good, but I must have written at least 200,000 words so far. For a long time I couldn't get the thing straight. I kept getting dissatisfied with the first 30,000 words and starting again. Today I reached Page 254 of my typescript, and all up to

90

there now looks all right. It really reads as if I had written it straight off without a pause.

While on the subject of writing, don't you find that the chief difficulty is getting the love story set? Boy meets girl. Right. But what happens then? I'm gradually assembling a plot where a rising young artist is sent for to Blandings Castle to paint a portrait. Of one of the family, he thinks, but when he gets there he finds that Lord Emsworth wants a portrait of his pig, to celebrate its winning the silver medal at the Agricultural Show in the Fat Pigs class. Artist, deeply offended, speaks disparagingly of pigs, and Lord E. kicks him out. On his way out he—the artist—sees a wonderful girl, falls in love at first sight, and realizes that he has now made it impossible for himself ever to enter the Blandings premises again. So he is obliged to hang around the place, seeking furtive meetings.

Now, then. Who is the girl? Why is she at Blandings? Has she a job? If so, what does she do?

Which reminds me of a story I once read—by S. J. Perelman? I can't remember—about a movie magnate who had a wonderful idea for a picture, and he sends to New York for an author, telling him when he arrives that every writer on the payroll has been stumped for three months by one detail in the story. Get that one small detail and the thing will be set, and I'm relying on you, he says.

"We fade in on a foggy street in London," he says, "and there's a guy dragging himself along through the fog, a Lon Chaney type guy, all twisted and crippled up. He comes to a colossal house in Berkeley Square and lets himself in with a latchkey, and he's in a gorgeous hall full of Chinese rugs and priceless pictures, and the minute he's inside he straightens up, takes off his harness, and unties his leg. Then we truck with him through a door, and he's like in a hospital corridor, and he pulls on rubber gloves and an operating gown and he goes into a room where there's ten, fifteen beautiful dames chained to the wall with prac'lly nothing on. We follow him to a bench that's full of test tubes and scientific stuff, and he grabs a hypodermic needle and he goes around laughing like a hyena and jabbing it into these beautiful dames. And that's where,

91

like I was telling you, you gotta figure out this one thing: *What kind of a business is this guy in?*"

Do you know what was one of the most interesting periods in history? The year 1822 in France, when the ex-officers of the Grande Armée were plotting to overthrow the Government and put Napoleon's son on the throne. I'm reading a book called *Les Demi-Soldes* (The Half-Pay Officers) by Desparbes (which sounds like the sort of name you give the characters in your stories). It's thrilling.

> *Royal Picardy Hotel*
> *Le Touquet*
> *France*
> *August 2, 1934*

Dear Bill,

Thanks for yours. I'm glad the novel is coming out well.

The big item of news is that we have bought a house here. Oddly enough, the only reason I came to Le Touquet was because I was writing the *Anything Goes* musical with Guy Bolton, and he isn't keen on working in Paris, so I said, All right, we'll meet halfway; I'll come to Le Touquet.

At first I didn't like the place much, and then it began to get me, and it struck both Ethel and me that as regards situation it was the ideal spot, only two hours from England by boat and only two and a half hours from Paris. We shall not be moving in, I suppose, till next spring, as the house wants fixing up.

Your *Ship in the Fanlight* arrived this morning, and I'm looking forward to reading it tonight in bed. They have given you a very good jacket this time.

I am now faced with a difficult job—a 16,000-word story for the New York *Herald Tribune*, to run in four parts. A short story is simple, and so is a 30,000-word novelette, but this in-between length is trying. I haven't room to build up an elaborate plot, and yet the story mustn't be thin and must have at least a passable curtain for each installment. Oh well, I suppose it will come.

Hutchinsons have sent me the *Century of Humour*, which I am billed as having edited. I put it like that because somebody in the office—probably the office boy—has shoved in without consulting me a whole lot of stories which I did not select, most of which are simply awful, notably a perfectly gruesome effort by Conan Doyle called "The Parish Magazine." Where they dug it up, I can't imagine. It's probably some very early thing of his which he hoped had been forgotten. But I do think they have a nerve, giving the impression that these ghastly exhibits were chosen by me. Not that it really matters a damn, of course. Your *Interlude in a Quiet Life* looks very good.

Low Wood
Le Touquet
October 5, 1934

Dear Bill,

I have been meaning to write to you for weeks, but I have been working on the 16,000-word story for the N. Y. *Herald Tribune*. I finished it this morning, after much sweat.

Thanks for the ideas for stories. (I'll send you some as soon as I can.) That one about sitting down in the chair that wasn't there is funny all right, but it's too like an *S.E.P.* story by Nunnally Johnson called *There Ought to Be a Law*, a terrific thing about a wife who could keep moving the furniture, so that in the big scene the husband, coming home worn out after a hard day at the office, chucks himself into bed in the dark, to find that the bed has been shifted to another corner of the room. Husband, furious, assaults wife, is arrested, and comes up in court. He explains that he was angry with his wife for persisting in moving the furniture, and the judge, the lawyers, the jury, and the policemen all start telling how *their* wives keep moving the furniture, and he gets everybody's sympathy and is acquitted without a stain on his character.

Why don't we do some stories together under a pseudonym? I've been brooding on the one you sent me, "The Old House." I believe that if one got a slightly different angle on it, it would go.

Do you remember the story? Young American wife shown over English country house by shabby old man, who turns out to be the owner. Arthur Morrison once did a very good one where a caller was shown over house by bloke who had just murdered the owner, whose body was lying in next room. Couldn't we do something on those lines?

I am very fit. The air here is wonderful, and I have to go and fetch the English papers every day from Paris Plage, which means a four-mile walk, so, what with taking the dogs for runs and generally messing about, I suppose I do a steady fifty miles a week. I notice the difference in my condition very much. In London my four-mile walk used to leave me not exactly tired but having had all I wanted, but here I hardly feel it.

Lady Dudley (used to be Gertie Millar at the Gaiety) lives a few doors off us and when she went to England asked me to exercise her Dalmatian occasionally. Well, of course, after I had taken it with me for two days to Paris Plage for the papers, it regarded this walk as a fixed ceremony. The day I had to go to Lille, I hear it refused all food and would not be comforted.

Low Wood
Le Touquet
December 4, 1934

Dear Bill,

I finished *The Luck of the Bodkins* on November 20, and ever since then have been in a sort of coma. Do you get like that after a big bout of work?

As a matter of fact, my present collapse is the result of a strain that has gone on now for almost six months. While in the middle of *The Luck of the Bodkins* and just beginning to see my way through it, I had to break off and start working on that musical comedy, *Anything Goes*, with Howard Lindsay, the director. We toiled all through that blazing weather in Paris, and then we came down here and started all over again with Guy Bolton.

Well, I eventually got back to the Bodkin novel again, and then I got the commission for the novelette for the *Herald Tribune*, to be done in a hurry. So I started sweating at that, and just as I was in the middle of it, a cable came from America from Vinton Freedley, the *Anything Goes* manager, saying that the stuff which Guy and I had sent over wouldn't do and that he was calling in Howard Lindsay and a friend to rewrite it. We had laid the scene on an ocean liner in danger in mid-ocean, and a few days after the delivery of the script the "Morro Castle" tragedy happened, which of course made our script as it stood impossible.

I got the novelette finished and sent it over, but was naturally not feeling confident about it after the debacle by the complete failure of the Bolton-Wodehouse comedy in London, because though it was a commission I wouldn't have felt able to take the money for the thing if they didn't want it, and for weeks I heard nothing.

Meanwhile, *The Luck of the Bodkins* was coming out with great difficulty, and then suddenly everything came right. My arrangement about *Anything Goes* was that I was to get 2 per cent of the gross if I was able to go to New York and attend rehearsals, but if I couldn't I was to give up ½ of 1 per cent. So I was looking on it all the time as a 1½ per cent job, which is the ordinary musical comedy royalty.

You can imagine my relief when I found that the rewriting wasn't going to affect my royalty very much. Russel Crouse, who was doing the rewriting with Lindsay, had agreed to do the work for ½ of 1 per cent, so I am only down ¼ of 1 per cent on the normal royalty. Then we heard that the show was a huge success in Boston, and now it has been produced in New York and is the biggest hit for years and Cochran has bought it for London. I gather from the notices that all Guy's best ideas—the lady Evangelist, the mild gangster Number 13, and so on—have been used in the new version. The arrangement we have with Lindsay and Crouse is that they have their names on the bill as authors in America, but the show will be played in England as "by Guy Bolton and P. G. Wodehouse."

Then I had a cable from the *Herald Tribune* which said, "Happy about Lord Havershot"—that was the name of the hero of the novelette—from which I inferred that it was all right. But I do hate these ambiguous cables. I mean, the editor might quite easily have written "Not happy" and the French postal officials might have cut out the word "Not" as not seeming to them important. Finally, however, a letter arrived, just about the time I heard the news of the success of the show, saying that they liked the story.

By that time I was struggling with the last chapters of the Bodkin book. Usually when I get to the last fifty pages of a novel, it begins to write itself, but this time everything went wrong and I had to grope my way through it at the rate of two pages of typescript a day. I began to feel superstitious about it and to think that if ever I could get it finished my luck would be in. On November 19 I was within four pages of the end and suddenly all the lights in the house went out and stayed out. Still, I finished it next day, and it is pretty good, I think. Frightfully long—362 pages of typescript —it must be over 100,000 words.

All this, added to the fact that Ethel has gone to London and it has been raining from the moment she left, has left me pretty limp. I suppose I shall be all right in a day or two.

Have you been following public-school football form this year? I have never known it so in and out.

> Bedford 30, Dulwich nil
> Dulwich nil, Haileybury 3
> Haileybury 9, Bedford 5
> Haileybury 5, Tonbridge 3
> Dulwich 11, Tonbridge nil

Dulwich beat Mill Hill, Mill Hill beat Brighton, Brighton beat Dulwich.

⟿⟾

The feverish interest I took in the football of my old school during these years when Civilization was showing every disposition to crash at any moment will lead many critics to look on me as a bad case of arrested mental development. And I would say they are probably right, were it not that some of our brightest minds have resembled me in that respect.

I remember lunching with Lord Birkenhead (F. E. Smith) once, and my opening remark "Well, Birkenhead, and how are politics these days?" left him listless. He merely muttered something about politics being all right and crumbled bread. But when I said, "Tell me, my dear fellow—I have often wanted to ask you—what came unstuck at Oxford in 1893 or whenever it was? Why was it that you didn't get your football blue?" his eyes lit up and he talked for twenty minutes without stopping, telling me how good he had been and giving me no chance to tell him what I did to opposing school teams in 1899.

This conversation, I should mention, took place in 1928. Footballers, like elephants, never forget.

P.G.W.

Low Wood
Le Touquet
January 23, 1935

Dear Bill,

When I got to Page 100 of your *Voyage Without End*, I rushed to my typewriter and wrote a letter to Arthur Waugh, the head of Chapman & Hall, raving about the book. As I don't know him, this will probably cause him to reject the thing immediately. Still, I meant well.

I think it's an absolute masterpiece. It's the only book I've read for years that did really take me out of myself into another atmosphere, so that I got the sense of coming back to another world when I finished reading. I just lived on that ship. What Ivor Nicholson's reader can be suffering from, to say that those characters aren't real, defeats me. There isn't one of them that you can't visualize with perfect clearness as you read.

One of the best tips for writing a play, so Guy tells me, is "Never let them sit down"—i.e., keep the characters buzzing about without a pause—and that is just what you have done here.

There isn't a moment till you come to the end of Part One where you can stop reading. You always feel there is something just around the corner.

Let's see what Chapman & Hall do. If they fail, I'll write to Tresham Lever, who is Thornton Butterworth, or E. V. Lucas, who runs Methuen.

I'll tell you one thing. From now on in your novels let yourself go. For magazines one more or less has to study the public, but not for novel publication. I believe there are two ways of writing novels. One is mine, making the thing a sort of musical comedy without music and ignoring real life altogether; the other is going right deep down into life and not caring a damn. The ones that fail are the ones where the writer loses his nerve and says, "My God! I can't write this. I must tone it down."

If you will send me a copy of *Greenside Island*, I'll ship it off to young Lorimer at the *Post*, telling him that it was submitted before, but that you have rewritten it. I gather that he has taken Costain's place, and Costain was the man who read it before. Costain is now eastern editor of Fox Films—a good job, I suppose, if you stay in it; but I wouldn't trust myself to a movie company. You dine with the president on Monday and he tells you you're the greatest thing since sliced bread, and on Tuesday morning you get a letter from him saying you're fired. But I should imagine Costain has a long contract.

Here's an idea you might use. I see a man at Ascot with a rich-looking but obviously unpleasant wife. I pity him, and you, who know him, tell me he is one of the happiest men of your acquaintance. You tell me his story. The point is that he's in love with a *house*. He is of hardish-up family, went to school in some awful suburb where he lived—not Dulwich, as Dulwich is too pleasant. He had some distant cousins who owned a lovely country house. Out of pity they used to have him to stay for two weeks in his summer holidays, and those two weeks were his real life. He worshiped the house—I mean really worshiped. It was the core of his whole inner life.

Then there came the war. The distant cousins lost all their sons and, in addition, went broke. (Note: He stopped going to stay at the house when he was seventeen, when he went into an office, so it has remained a remote Paradise to him all this time.) Some profiteers bought the house, and a chain of circumstances—he might be in the profiteer's office—brought him into contact with profiteer's daughter, a spoiled, awful girl.

You will have to give the chap some quality of attraction, good looks or something, because the daughter wants him and insists on having him—presumably against parental opposition—and he marries her just because it will mean that he can get back to the house. So there he is when I meet him. He is snubbed by the parents, and the girl nags him, because her brief infatuation is over and she realizes that she has landed herself with a nobody as a husband. He has a rotten time as far as his outward life goes, but he is perfectly happy. He has the house and can putter about and dream.

I couldn't begin to handle it myself—right out of my line—but you might be able to make something of it. It has something of the quality of your *The Rose House.*

The Dorchester
London W. 1
February 4, 1935

Dear Bill,

I've just had the foulest week of my career. It included two visits to the dentist, a cold in the head, the opening of Crockford's Club (one of those ghastly functions where you're invited for ten o'clock and don't have any dinner because you think supper will be served the moment you arrive and then don't get any supper), an interviewer who caught me just as the cold was at its worst, and finally a cocktail party to celebrate the publication of a young author's new book, which I got let in for owing to temperamental inability to say no when asked to do anything. (Weak character, very weak.)

I confidently expected that the cocktail party would make me plumb the depths, and it did. It seemed to take me into a new and dreadful world. Can you imagine giving a party to celebrate the publication of a book? With a mob of your young friends, mostly fairies, twittering all over the place screaming "Oh, Lionel!" and you being photographed holding the book and looking down at it with a smirk? Gosh! Dumas was the boy. When he had finished a novel, he kept right on sitting and started another. No cocktail parties and photographers for him. (Incidentally, why are young English authors so uniformly bloody? American ones aren't. I think it's Oxford that does it.)

Well, all that was bad enough, but on top of it came the news that the *Saturday Evening Post* don't want *The Luck of the Bodkins*—my first rejection in America in twenty-one years. It was a stunning blow. I had come to look on myself so much as the *Post*'s favorite son, to whom they could refuse nothing, that I felt like a child who has run to its mother for a slice of cake and been met with a solid kick in the pants.

I have now reread the book as critically as if it were someone else's—all right, someone's else, if you prefer it—and I see what's wrong. It's at least 25,000 words too long. I had such a good farcical plot in this one that I got all hopped up and felt that it wasn't possible to give 'em too much of this superb stuff, with the result that every scene was elaborated till it lost its grip. I've started cutting and I now reach on Page 45 a situation which in the original I got to on Page 100. That's 15,000 words out for a start. I expect to cut 30,000, and after I've done that I'm sure I shall be able to sell it somewhere, probably to the *Red Book*, who have been asking me for a serial. But it's pretty galling to think that after earning one's living as a writer for so long one can make a blunder like that. It just shows that you can never relax your vigilance for a second at this game.

I've just had a review of my last book in some provincial paper, criticizing in an adverse spirit a scene which is not in the book at all, but in Eric Linklater's *Ripeness Is All*.

Dear Bill,

I have been at the above address since February 24. I return to Low Wood on Saturday.

Your letter, forwarded on to me from Le Touquet, reached me last night. I am very bucked that Chapman & Hall have taken *Voyage Without End*. I must say I feel a bit uneasy about that huge cut they want to make, and particularly when you say that they have cut out 30,000 words already. Of course, your script ran to nearly 140,000 words and one can understand them wanting to shorten it a bit, but I think you ought to be in sole control of any cutting that has to be done.

Can you hang on for a few days, till I can get back to Le Touquet and read the story again? You say you would like the script at once, but the only living soul at Low Wood is a Yugoslavian butler, and if I wrote to him to mail it to you, it would probably result in your receiving either (a) the MS of *The Luck of the Bodkins* or (b) a handsomely bound volume of the Encyclopaedia Britannica.

Why don't you do a series about Captain Shuffley? He seems to me as good as W. W. Jacobs' Bob Pretty. I see him as a chap who might have adventure after adventure, doing the most gallant things but always making a bit out of them. You know what I mean—he saves a girl from a bunch of thugs in a low-down café in Buenos Aires, laying them out in droves, and you find at end that his main motive in starting the big rescue scene was that he hadn't any money to pay his bill and wanted a way of creating a diversion.

Have you ever noticed how if you are expecting an important telegram, some absolutely unimportant one arrives? I remember in 1922 when *The Beauty Prize* was put on at the Winter Garden, I sailed for New York the day it opened and, of course, expected a wireless about how it had gone and what the notices were like. On the first day out along came a wireless and I tore it open. It was from Leslie Henson, wishing me Bon Voyage.

The same thing has happened now. I am all in a twitter about the fate of some stuff I sent over to New York. I got a letter from my agent saying that the editor of the *Red Book* liked the stories, but that a snag had arisen. The president of the *Red Book* company, which also owns *McCall's*, is sore because in 1922 I contracted to do six short stories for *McCall's* and never delivered them! I'm blowed if I know how that happened, but apparently it did, and the president has been brooding on it ever since. In his letter my agent said it rather looked as if we may have to shade our price a bit as compensation.

Well, as anything I get out of America nowadays with this income-tax dispute going on is like a bone sneaked from a dog, I cabled, "Close deal at any price you can get and cable at once." Sure enough, a telegram arrived next night. It was from Gertie Millar at Le Touquet, thanking me for having exercised her Dalmatian dog in her absence.

> *Low Wood*
> *Le Touquet*
> *March 28, 1935*

Dear Bill,

The sun has broken through the clouds. My New York agent cables that he has sold *The Luck of the Bodkins* and three short stories to the *Red Book*. $25,000 for the Bodkins as against the $40,000 the *Post* would have paid if they had taken it, but what of it? Oo là là, as we say over here.

What asses Pekes are! We took Winky to Paris, leaving Boo, the other Peke, behind. When we brought her back, was there a joyful reunion? No, sir. Each poor fish had completely forgotten the other, and each, seeing a stranger in her home, prepared to fight to the death. They had six fights in the first ten minutes but have now settled down. One of the fights was the funniest thing you ever saw. I had put my typewriter case down in a corner and Winky was behind it. Boo came up in front and they both reared up on their hind legs and stood with their noses touching, snarling and growling but unable to get at each other. This went on for about five minutes.

Next day that hound Boo nearly got killed. Ethel and I were walking on left side of road. Two girls on bicycles came along on right side. Boo dashed across and gave chase, spilling one girl. I went and picked her up, and Boo legged it after the other one, spilling her also. I was twenty yards behind when I saw car coming, and at that moment Boo swerved to the left. I gave a yell and the car stopped with the wheel right over her. Another revolution and she would have been squashed. She then trotted to Ethel and lay on her back, which is her idea of passing off a delicate situation.

Just had a testing job—reading the proofs of the *Mulliner Omnibus* book. 864 pages! It humbled me a good deal, as the stories didn't seem funny. Still, I suppose nothing would, if you read 864 pages of it straight off.

I can't get an idea for a novel. Maddening, as except for that I am fixed so solidly for the coming year, for there will be four companies of *Anything Goes* playing, not counting the London one, and I have an original play for Ralph Lynn—*The Inside Stand*—and an adaptation coming on in London, and I am well ahead with short stories. But all is useless unless I can get started on a novel.

Oh, this will interest you. When I last saw Askew, he said why doesn't Townend stick to sea stories, adding that one single bookseller in Glasgow sold a thousand copies of the half-crown edition of *The Tramp*. Of course, this is a hell of a time to tell you this, when you are in the middle of a non-sea novel, but as a guide for the future apparently what they want from you is sea stuff.

Enclosed will give you a laugh. Me and Mussolini!

A letter from the president of the International Mark Twain Society gives the explanation of "Me and Mussolini."

Webster Groves
Missouri
March 11, 1935

Dear Mr. Wodehouse.

In recognition of your outstanding and lasting contribution to the happiness of the world, it gives us much pleasure to offer you the Mark Twain Medal. The list enclosed will show you to whom the Medal has been given in the past.

With all good wishes,

Yours sincerely,
Cyril Clemens

The list included Mussolini.
In October 1936 Plum went to Hollywood for the second time.

W.T.

1315 Angelo Drive
Beverly Hills, Cal.
Nov. 7, 1936

Dear Bill,

Well, here we are, settled in a house up at the top of a mountain, surrounded by canyons in which I'm told rattlesnakes abound, and employing a protection agency to guard the place at nights. The latter is a common thing in these parts. Generally, when you go out to dinner with someone, a uniformed figure bounds out of the bushes and holds you up with a gun till you have satisfied him that you're there by invitation. We looked at a lot of houses in the valley part of Beverly Hills, where we were before, but couldn't find one that Ethel liked, so we took this one, which is a lovely place with a good pool, but, as I say, remote. We have one house across the road from us—Nelson Eddy's—and another about half a mile further up the mountain, but everything else is wilderness and rattlesnakes and tarantulas. The butler killed two black widow spiders in the garden yesterday, and last night and this morning the following episodes occurred. We were taking the dogs for a stroll after dinner, and Wonder disappeared. We went back and found her playing with a tarantula on the drive. And this morning when I came out from my swim, I heard her gruffling at something on the steps of the pool, and there was another tarantula, bigger than the first one. So life is never dull.

I am having quite a good time, but it isn't as interesting as it was in 1930. Thalberg's death has made the place seem rather flat, though I like Sam Katz, for whom I am working. If you can believe it, they have put me on to *Rosalie* again. I did think I had heard the last of that dame when I left Hollywood six years ago, but no, they have been saving her up for me. "Dust off *Rosalie*" was the cry when they heard I was coming. Well, as the fellow said, there are no friends like old friends.

Before setting out for California, I went to see Lorimer at the *Saturday Evening Post*. He was very friendly, and said he would have taken *The Luck of the Bodkins* if it hadn't been so long and hadn't had a jewel-smuggling plot. He said he thought it a good story, which relieved my apprehensions that I might be slipping, but the *Post* couldn't countenance a serial which ended with the fellow sneaking a necklace through the Customs in the lining of his hat. My last *Post* contribution was a short story, "The Crime Wave at Blandings," and he paid me $2,000 and wrote me a letter asking if that was all right. I wrote back: "Dear Mr. Lorimer, I am so intensely spiritual that money means nothing to me, but I must confess that that $2,000 was a bit of a sock on the jaw, as I had been expecting $4,000." This apparently touched his heart, for the first thing he said to me when I came into the room was that he would give me $4,000 for it.

He seemed a little taken aback when I walked in, as he had not seen me since the days when I had thick black hair on my now bald head. Did I ever tell you about that? He bought *Something New*, and when I wrote *Uneasy Money*, he asked me to spend the weekend at his house, bringing the script with me. On the Sunday he curled up on the sofa and began to read the thing, with me sitting there pretending to be absorbed in a bound volume of the *Post* but really, of course, listening in anguish in the hope of hearing him laugh. Which presently he began to do, and after about half an hour he said: "I like this one better than the other." I never heard such beautiful words in my life. At the end of the first hour he said he would buy it if I would be satisfied with $5,000. Satisfied! I'd have taken $500. For *Something New* he had given me $3,500, and he told me it would have been $5,000, only he had had a row with my agent and wanted to score off him. Tough luck on a young writer to be caught in the middle of a feud like that, don't you think?

I've always thought that his buying *Something New* showed what a wonderful editor he was. Here was a story by an absolutely unknown author and a story, what is more, about life in England, a country he didn't like, but it amused him, so he decided without any hesitation that the public of the *Post* were jolly well going to be amused by it, too, and he didn't give a damn if they weren't.

I think the reason English magazines die off like flies is that the editors are wondering timidly all the time what their readers are going to like, and won't take a chance on anything that isn't on exactly the same lines as everything else they have ever printed. Lorimer has always had an unswerving faith in his own judgment. His attitude is "I like this story, and I don't care what anyone else thinks." That's how he has made the *Post* such a success. He is retiring from the editorship in January, to be succeeded by Wesley Stout.

On my way out I ran into Erd Brandt, who used to be your agent and is now the *Post* fiction editor. He spoke very highly of you and told me you were living in Brazil. I didn't tell him you weren't, because I thought you might want to do some stories for them with a strong Brazil nut interest and it would help if they thought you were a man who knew his Brazil nuts. They want to see your stuff. Brandt said they all remembered it and liked it.

1315 Angelo Drive
Beverly Hills, Cal.
December 28, 1936

Dear Bill,

Thanks for your long letter with all the news about Dulwich football. Very sad, losing to Haileybury. Somehow we never seem to get the breaks against them. The best game I ever played was against Haileybury in 1899. It resulted in a pointless draw, but I still swear I scored in the second half when we were all tumbling over one another on their line, only the referee didn't see eye to eye with me. I call it a very good performance beating St. Paul's. If they could take fifteen points off Bedford, they must be a good side.

(Incidentally, isn't it amazing that you and I, old buffers of fifty-five, with Civilization looking as if it were going to crash at any moment, can get all worked up about school football? It's really about the only thing I do get worked up about.)

I haven't finished my novel yet. That blasted *Rosalie* has been keeping me busy. I don't know if I told you, but the producer I am working under is none other than Bill McGuire. They made him a producer some months ago, a happy ending to his hand-to-mouth existence. After a lifetime of keeping one jump ahead of creditors, process servers, etc., it must give him a dazed feeling to have a steady job and a big salary. It's as if Ukridge suddenly found himself a bank president.

I am calling the novel *Summer Moonshine*, and it's one of those difficult ones where I can't just dash off an odd chapter at odd times. It needs concentration.

I have a short story coming out in *S.E.P.* week ending January 30, which they think is the best I have ever done. It was sent to the *Red Book* and they offered $2,000 for it, having given me $3,000 for my other ones. I refused this, and on landing in America called up the editor and asked him to return the story—having visited Lorimer the previous day and, as I believe I told you, got him to agree that he would pay $4,000 for any things of mine which he accepted. The *Red Book* editor raised the offer to $2,500, but I believed in the story so much that I turned him down, and am glad that I did, because the *Post* jumped at it. Title—"All's Well with Bingo."

We have now reached the rainy season here. Funny how one never minds rain in England, but in California it seems to upset everything.

1315 Angelo Drive
Beverly Hills, Cal.
March 7, 1937

Dear Bill,

I meant to send you a lot of clippings about the frosts in these parts, but forgot. Anyway, the gist is that we have had a foul winter and the valley below this house has been wrapped in a dense London fog for weeks because of the smudge pots they have been burning to try to save the lemon crops. Did smudge pots enter into your lemon life when you were in California, or was it always warm here then in winter? Lemons have been almost wiped out this year, and the latest local gag is about the New York man who came to Southern California for the winter—and found it.

Have you ever pondered on the importance of a name to a writer or actor? Up till the time when I wrote *Something New* I was labeling my stories "by P. G. Wodehouse" and getting nowhere, but the moment I called myself Pelham Grenville Wodehouse editors laid down the red carpet for me. I suppose they felt there would be something indecent about refusing a thing by a man with a name like that.

Out here, apparently, the name is even more important. Somebody was telling me the other day about Frank Lovejoy, the movie star, who for a time couldn't seem to click, and wondered why till one morning his agent explained it to him.

"We meet producer resistance," the agent told me, "on account of your name. The studio heads don't think it a suitable name for a movie star. What they want today is strong names, like Rock Bostock, Steel Ironside, and so on. Try to think of something."

"Tab Zanuch?"

"Not bad."

"Or Max Million?"

"Better still. That's got it."

A week later Mr. Lovejoy's telephone rang.

"Max Million speaking," he said.

"It is, is it?" said the agent, for it was he. "Well, it better not be. The trend has changed. They don't want strong names any more; they want *sincere* names."

"How do you mean, sincere names?"

"Well, like Abe Lincoln."

"Abe Washington?"

"Fine."

"Or Ike Roosevelt?"

"No, I think Abe Washington's better."

So Frank Lovejoy became Abe Washington, and all seemed well, but his contentment was short-lived. The agent called up again to say that there had been another shift in the party line and the trend now was toward *familiar* names like Clark Cooper and Alan Gable. And just as his client was wavering between Humphrey Ladd and Spencer Stewart he had another telephone call.

"There's been a further shake-up," the agent said. "What they want now is happy names suggestive of love and joy."

"How about Frank Lovejoy?"

"Swell," said the agent.

I always think you made a mistake in calling yourself W. Townend. It should have been Clarence Budington Rockaway.

I am in the middle of a four weeks' job on *A Damsel in Distress* for Fred Astaire. When R.K.O. bought the book, they gave it to one of their writers to adapt, and he turned out a script all about crooks—no resemblance to the novel. Then it struck them that it might be a good thing to stick to the story, so they chucked away the other script and called me in. I think it's going to be a good picture. We have the best director in Hollywood—George Stevens.

But what uncongenial work picture writing is. Somebody's got to do it, I suppose, but this is the last time they'll get me.

Just before I started in on the *Damsel*, I managed to get *Summer Moonshine* finished. Lorimer's son Graeme called on me about two weeks ago and took away the first 70,000 words, leaving me another 10,000 to do. What an efficient machine the *Saturday Evening Post* is. When Lorimer took over the editorship, he made it a fixed rule that on every manuscript that came into the office a decision should be given in seventy-two hours. This time, of course, with Graeme making a three-day train journey, they couldn't do that, but he left on a Friday, read the thing on the train, arrived Philadelphia Monday night, presumably went to the office Tuesday morning and gave the MS to somebody else, who must have read it Tuesday and given it to Stout, and Stout must have read it Wednesday, because on Thursday morning I got a telegram saying it had been accepted. I don't see how they can manage to be so quick. They get 75,000 MSS a year, all of which are read.

The most extraordinary thing happened. They bought it for $40,000 as usual, and then two days later Stout added on another $5,000 without—as far as I can ascertain—being asked to. Pretty lavish! Warms the cockles of the heart, that sort of thing.

❧

It occurs to me, reading over these letters, that there is a great deal about money in them, but I suppose that is unavoidable when an author is writing to another author. We pen-pushers, as a class, are businessmen. Shakespeare described the poet's eye as rolling in a fine frenzy from heaven to earth, from earth to heaven, but you will generally find that one corner of that eye is glued on the royalty returns, and it is the same with novelists and short story writers.

But I disagree with Dr. Johnson when he said that nobody but a blockhead ever wrote except for money. I should think it extremely improbable that anyone ever went into the trade of authorship solely with the idea of making money at it. What urges a writer to write is that he likes writing. Naturally, when he has written something, he wants to get as much for it as he can, but that is a very different thing from writing for money.

I should imagine that even the man who compiles a railroad time-table is thinking much more of what fun it all is than of the check he is going to get when he turns in the completed script. Watch his eyes sparkle as he puts a very small (a) against the line

    4:51 arr. 6:22

knowing that the reader will not notice it and turn to the bottom of the page, where it says

    (a) On Saturdays only

but will dash off with his suitcase and golf clubs all merry and bright, arriving in good time at the station on the afternoon of Friday. Money is the last thing such a writer has in mind.

                                                    P.G.W.

                                        1315 Angelo Drive
                                        Beverly Hills, Cal.
                                        March 24, 1937

Dear Bill,

        Metro-Goldwyn are not taking up my option, which ex-pires in another two weeks. I have had another flop with them. After working under Bill McGuire's eye for some time, I gradu-ally found myself being edged out. Eventually, the brass hats came out into the open and said they had wanted McGuire to write the thing by himself, all along. There seems to be a curse on M-G-M, as far as I am concerned.

    Since then, I have had a number of offers from other studios for one picture apiece. It seems pretty certain that in about two weeks I shall be working on my *Damsel in Distress*, which R.K.O. bought for Fred Astaire. George Gershwin will be doing the mu-sic and Ira the lyrics. Ira has done a superb lyric called "Stiff Up-per Lip" which will fit in perfectly, and another called "A Foggy Day in London Town." So nothing to worry about as regards the numbers.

    Interesting about your visit to the specialist. It's nice to know that your heart is all right. Isn't it difficult to get accustomed to the idea that one is now nearing the age when most people pack up and settle down? I am now exactly the same age as my father was when I left school, and I remember him as tottering to his armchair and settling in it for the day. That's one thing about being a writer: it does keep you young. Do you find you can't walk as far as you used to? I do out here, but in Le Touquet I used to do my seven miles without feeling it. I think it's mainly the California climate.

I can't fathom the mentality of Pekes. Yesterday Roland Young came to tea and sat on the sofa with Winky snuggling up to him on one side and Wonder the puppy on the other. The moment he got up and started to leave, both Pekes sprang down and attacked his ankles. You'd have thought they had never seen him before and had spotted him breaking in through a window.

Our butler got home last night tight as a drum and is still sleeping it off. Over here the help take every Thursday off, and he employed his holiday in getting thoroughly pickled.

Big strike now in the picture industry, which may close all the studios. That'll teach them not to take up my option.

Leaving Hollywood, Plum returned to Le Touquet and started work on a Jeeves novel entitled *The Code of the Woosters*, concerning which he wrote me in a chastened spirit some months later.

W.T.

Low Wood
Le Touquet
November 22, 1938

Dear Bill,

Hell! I've done it again! Though not so badly, thank goodness, as with *The Luck of the Bodkins*.

I sent the *Post* the first 50,000 words of *The Code of the Woos-*

ters, and they like it, but they feel that the early part needs cutting. "Too many stage waits" was what Brandt said, and when I looked at it, I saw he was right. Here is the layout as I had it.

1. Bertie goes to see his Aunt Dahlia. She tells him to go and buy flowers for Aunt Agatha, who is in hospital.
2. Bertie goes back to his flat and Aunt Dahlia phones to say she has another job for him—which will necessitate visit to an antique shop.
3. Bertie goes to flower shop and gets into trouble.
4. Bertie goes back to his flat and tells Jeeves about it.
5. Bertie goes to antique shop and gets into more trouble.

Now, can you believe it, I'd written that part half a dozen times and hadn't spotted that the flower shop scene wasn't necessary and just held up the action and that the thing ought to run thus:

1. Bertie goes to Aunt Dahlia. She tells him to go to antique shop.
2. Bertie goes to antique shop.

It cuts out fifteen pages without losing anything of value. Why on earth I kept taking Bertie back to the flat, where nothing happened, I can't imagine. Do you think that when one reaches our present age one loses one's power of self-criticism and just drools on like a club bore?

How vitally important it is, when you're doing a story, to get it started right. A book's different from a play. If you're in a theater watching a play and the first act's slow, you don't leave; you sit on, hoping for better things. But if you're reading a novel and the opening pages make you yawn, you just drop it.

Did you ever read an old book called *Helen's Babies*, about a young bachelor getting saddled with his sister's two kids? The *Ladies' Home Journal* editor has got the idea that a splendid modern version could be made, and he has offered me $45,000 if I will do it. I don't think there's anything in it. When *Helen's Babies* was published, all you had to do was to get the central idea and then have a monotonous stream of incidents showing the kids causing trouble. But surely that sort of thing wouldn't go now. In any case, while I suppose I could dish out something that might get by, if I brooded on it, it wouldn't satisfy me. I'll never do a story, however much I'm offered, unless I feel I can make it good.

Just heard from a bloke called Douglas Beale, registrar of the University, that they want to give me an honorary D. Litt. at Oxford. I said, Right ho, I'd be there; but I'm not looking forward to it. They tell me you have to wear a cap and gown (with scarlet facings) and parade through the streets in them. I expect to feel like thirty cents.

On Wednesday, June 21, 1939, at the Encaenia at Oxford University, Plum—on this occasion Mr. Pelham Grenville Wodehouse—received the degree of D. Litt.

In its report of the proceedings in the Sheldonian the *Times* in its issue of June 22 said:

> Last, but in the opinion of the University far from least, came Mr. P. G. Wodehouse, whom the Public Orator presented as *festivum caput—Petroniumne dicam an Terentium nostrum?* The *PUBLIC ORATOR* fittingly marked almost his last public appearance, and delighted his audience by a passage of Horatian hexameters, an exemplum of his own *urbana felicitas*, in which he not only paid tribute to the kindly temper and finished style of Mr. Wodehouse's work, but also achieved the difficult task of presenting or suggesting in Latin the familiar figures of Bertie Wooster and Jeeves and Mr. Mulliner and Lord Emsworth and the Empress of Blandings and Psmith and even the Honourable Augustus Fink-Nottle and the love life of the newts.

In the same number of the *Times* there appeared the following verses:

D. LITT., 1939
Dear Mr. Wodehouse, who'll applaud your D. Litt.?
Jeeves, Mr. Mulliner, Bertie, Psmith, Aunt Dahlia,
Gussie Fink-Nottle, Tuppy, both the Freddies.
        Threepwood and Widgeon,
Sam the Sudden, Ronnie, Empress and Lord Emsworth,
Stinker Pinker, Biscuit, Monty, Lotus Blossom,

Beach, Beefy Bingham, gay old Gally Threepwood,
    Albert E. Peasmarsh.
Who'll look austerely? Lady Constance Keeble,
Baxter, Sir Roderick, all the tribe of Parsloe,
Roderick Blackshorts (Eulalie in Secret).
    Tilbury, Pilbeam.
Ruler unquestioned of the Land of Laughter,
Scholar, creator, lord of apt quotation,
Master of words, of things yet unattempted,
    Thanks, Dr. Wodehouse.

Of Plum a leader-writer in the June 22 issue of the *Times* said:

> —but there is no question that in making Mr. P. G. Wodehouse
> a doctor of letters the University has done the right and popular
> thing. Everyone knows at least some of his many works and has
> felt all the better for the gaiety of his wit and the freshness of
> his style. Style goes a long way in Oxford; indeed the purity of
> Mr. Wodehouse's style was singled out for particular praise in
> the public Orator's happy Horatian summing up of Mr. Wode-
> house's qualities and achievements.

A few weeks later war broke out and Plum was captured by the
Germans in Le Touquet and interned. It was not until 1945 that I
heard from him again.

W.T.

1940-1961

Hotel Lincoln
Rue Bayard
Paris
February 5, 1945

Dear Bill,

At last I am able to drop you a line. My friend Malcolm Muggeridge is leaving for England this week and will mail it. He will be in London about ten days, I think, so if you have time to write me a letter, you could send it to me care of him. I will add his London address in a postscript, as I shall not know it till I see him this afternoon. I am longing to get a letter from you, telling me all the news.

I have only recently settled in at above address. As you have probably seen in the papers, I was pinched as a suspicious character by the French and spent four days at the Palais de Justice, getting very matey with the *inspecteurs* and making good progress with a novel I'm writing called *Uncle Dynamite*. If *Uncle Dynamite* ever gets published and you happen to run across a copy, turn to Chapter Nine, the one that begins, "It is a characteristic of England's splendid police force. . . ." The whole of that chapter was written in the *inspecteurs'* room with the boys crowding round to see how I was getting along.

On the evening of the fourth day I was released and Malcolm drove Ethel and me down to Barbizon, about thirty miles from Paris, in the most awful blizzard. When we got to the Barbizon hotel, we found it was strictly a summer hotel—no carpets, no heating, and no running water, owing to frozen pipes. And, to make things more difficult, Malcolm absentmindedly drove off with my suitcase, leaving me what I stood up in. I slept for two nights in my clothes, plus a heavy overcoat, and still felt chilly. He then sent a minion down with my things, after which I was all right. We settled down and had a very good time for three weeks, and then the hotel was requisitioned by SHAEF, so we are back in Paris. It is very pleasant, though living conditions are getting tougher every day, and I don't like the look of the Seine, which may burst its banks at any moment. Still, Paris is always Paris.

(I was just writing this, when an air-raid warning sounded. I thought all that sort of thing was over in these parts. Still, there it is. I'll let you know how the matter develops.)

Where was I? Oh, yes, Paris. Quite a city. I have been hobnobbing a good deal with the American soldiers, who spend their time in little sort of fortified edifices up and down the Champs Élysées and I should imagine find it pretty dull. Anyway, they always seem glad to have a chat. It's good to hear an American voice again.

The air raid is still apparently in progress, as there has been no all clear, but nothing seems to be happening. Do tell me, when you write, about your work since the war started. Is the *Strand* still going? Have you read ("all clear" just gone) Hesketh Pearson's life of Conan Doyle? Very interesting. It's curious to find what small prices he got for books which are famous. I can't remember offhand, but I think he got $600 for the complete American rights of *The White Company*.

Uncle Dynamite is coming out quite well, even though I no longer have the *inspecteurs* to encourage me. They were all so interested in my work that I felt under an obligation to give of my best. It was the same thing in camp, where I used to sit on my typewriter case with the machine balanced on a suitcase and work away at *Money in the Bank* with two German soldiers standing behind me with rifles, breathing down the back of my neck. They seemed fascinated by this glimpse into the life literary, and I expected them at any moment to ask me if I worked regular hours or just waited for inspiration.

Did you happen to see a thing by George Orwell called "In Defense of P. G. Wodehouse"? (It was in his book *Dickens, Dali and Others*, if that's the right title.) In it he says that my "Indiscretion" (the broadcasts) gave a good propaganda opening to the left-wingers of England because "it was a chance to expose a wealthy parasite." Had it ever occurred to you that that is how authors are regarded in England? You, me, Shakespeare, all of us, just parasites. (Have you read any good parasites lately?) It's very different in France. Seeing me hammering out my wholesome fiction, the *inspecteurs* used to treat me with reverence. For two pins (*épingles*) they would have called me "maître."

⁓⤬⁓

I wrote two novels in camp, *Money in the Bank* and *Full Moon*. Conditions for composition were not too good. I wrote them at the rate of about a page a day in a room where fifty men were playing ping-pong and talking and singing. On an average morning I would get from fifteen to twenty ping-pong balls on the side of the head as I sat molding my prose. It made it a little hard to concentrate at times.

As I was starting Chapter Thirteen of *Money in the Bank*, the library was opened and I was made president. The president of a camp library must not be confused with the librarian. The librarian does the rough work, like handing out books and entering them in a ledger; the president presides. I, for instance, used to look in once a day and say "Everything OK?" and go away again. It was amazing how it helped.

Being president of the library, I became entitled to a padded cell all to myself. (The building where we internees were housed at Tost in Upper Silesia was a lunatic asylum.) I was able to write the remainder of *Money in the Bank* and the whole of *Full Moon* in a peaceful seclusion disturbed only by the sound of musicians practicing trombones, violins, etc., in the interests of the Entertainment Committee or lecturers lecturing on Chaucer and Beowulf under the auspices of the Committee for Education. All that I know of Beowulf today I owe to these lectures. Must have been a nice guy, from what I could catch of what the lecturer was saying.

It was not until we got to Tost that we enjoyed these amenities. Our previous ports of call—Loos Prison, Liége Barracks, and the Citadel of Huy—had all been on the tough side, notably the last named, where we had too little food and too many parades. I remember a parade being called to inform us that stealing was forbidden.

We paraded when told to—which was about ten times a day—but we liked to do it in our own way. One of the sergeants wanted us to go through the motions smartly, with lots of snap. "Come on, boys," he seemed to be saying. "Get the Carnival spirit. Switch on the charm. Give us the old personality." He actually suggested that we should come on parade at the double. When we were convinced that we had really heard what we thought we had heard, we looked at one another with raised eyebrows and asked our linguist to explain to this visionary that in order to attend parade we had to climb twenty-seven steep stone steps. It was unreasonable, we felt, to expect us to behave like mountain goats on a diet of crackers about the size of aspirin tablets and one small mug of thin soup a day.

"Try to make him understand," we urged the linguist, "that it is pretty darned creditable of us getting on parade at all. Tell him he has sized us up all wrong. We are elderly internees, most of us with corns and swollen joints, not Alpine climbers. If we are supposed to be youths who bear 'mid snow and ice a banner with the strange device, Excelsior, there ought to be Saint Bernard dogs stationed here and there, dispensing free brandy. Ask him if he expects us to yodel."

Our linguist put these points, and the man saw reason. Only once during our stay at the Citadel of Huy did our iron front break down. That was when a spruce young lieutenant, a stranger to us, took over and electrified us by shouting "Achtung!" in a voice like someone calling the cattle home across the Sands of Dee. It startled us so much that we sprang to attention like a Guards regiment.

But we were waiting for him in the evening. He shouted "Achtung!" again and didn't get a ripple.

Episodes like these jarred the sensitive soul, of course, but, taken by and large, internment was not so very terrible. The most shattering thing that happened to me was my shower bath in Loos Prison. If you are in the coop at Loos, you all troop up once a week to the top floor and take a tepid shower under the supervision of a prison official. You remove your clothes and queue up, and when you reach the head of the line the official slips a dab of soft soap into your hand and you go under the water. And where I made my mistake was in supposing that I had lots of time.

I am one of those cautious shower-bathers who put a toe in first and then, if all seems well, another toe, and, in a word, sort of lead up to the thing: and it became apparent almost immediately that what the man up top wanted to see was something in the nature of an imitation of forked lightning striking a mountain torrent. The result was that just as I had soft-soaped myself all over and was hovering on the brink, my feet, as the poet Suckling said, like little mice stealing in and out, he informed me that my time was up and told me to put my clothes on and go back to my cell.

I don't know if any of you present here tonight have ever put your clothes on over a foundation of soft soap and tried to wash it off at the cold tap without a sponge, but it is one of those experiences that test you. You come out of it a deeper, graver man, not perhaps so fond of French prison officials as you used to be, but with a wonderful feeling of having your manhood tried in the furnace and the realization that life is stern and earnest and that we are not put into the world for pleasure alone.

P.G.W.

Hotel Lincoln
Rue Bayard
Paris
April 6, 1945

Dear Bill,

I was very interested in your long letter about your books. I wish I could get hold of them. The last of yours I read was *Sink and Be Damned,* which I thought awfully good. What a nuisance the paper shortage is. It must be maddening to sell out before publication and then not be able to follow it up because there is no paper for another printing. I sympathize with your trouble with the printers and their queries. The American cousins of these birds read the proofs of the *S. E. Post,* and I used to spend hours writing sarcastic replies in the margin. I remember in *Quick Service* they queried the grammar of some remark made by a barmaid in a moment of extreme agitation, and I wrote a long essay on the margin pointing out that when an English barmaid is deeply stirred her syntax often goes a bit cockeyed. Futile, of course.

Talking of *Quick Service,* Grimsdick of Jenkins sent me a copy and Duff Cooper, who had become Ambassador to France, swiped it. It had to pass through his hands before I could get it, and it didn't pass through his ruddy hands. He stuck to it like glue. It's nice, of course, to know that he's one of the fans, but I wish he had passed the book on after he had done with it, as I wanted to reread it. So it's no good your sending me any of your books while he is still around. Probably he is one of your warmest admirers and would whoop with joy at the chance of adding your latest to his shelves at no expense to himself. He hasn't approached me yet to autograph that copy of *Quick Service,* but no doubt he will before long. I think the French politicians he mixed with would be well advised to put their books in a stout box and sit on the lid, and I should imagine they do.

I finished *Uncle Dynamite* last Sunday. What with one thing and another, it has taken me exactly a year to write, but I think the results are good. It was one of those difficult stories where you get everything into a tangle and then straighten it all out in the last chapter, and all the way through I was saying to myself: "Well, it's all right so far, but that last chapter is going to let the whole thing down." But, fortunately, the last chapter came out all right.

I've been reading Mark Twain's letters. Very interesting. He thought an enormous lot of W. D. Howells' books. Have you read any of them? I have taken *The Rise of Silas Lapham* out of the American library here, and it certainly is good. It was written in 1885 but reads quite like a modern novel. I wish I could get hold of some of Raymond Chandler's things. They sound, from what you say, just the kind of books I like. (Did you know that he was at school at Dulwich, but after our time?) Something new occasionally creeps through to Paris, but it's very difficult to find anything except prewar books. I have just got Peter Cheyney's last, and it's about an inch thick and printed on a sort of brown paper, and the price is nine shillings and sixpence. Before the war no publisher would have put out a shilling edition like that. I think the paper shortage is worse than the food shortage. Here in Paris the papers don't come out on Mondays. One week the nonappearance day was shifted to Wednesday for some reason, with the result that the papers were not able to report the death of Hitler, which must have annoyed them.

I'm having trouble with the American income-tax people. They have dug back to 1923 and claim that I made no return that year. I have absolutely no means of proving that I did, as all the records disappeared ages ago, but I must have done, for I was in America in 1923 doing shows—*Sitting Pretty* was one of them—and you can't get on a boat at New York and sail to England unless you can show documentary evidence that you have paid your income tax. It's an awful nuisance, and I wouldn't have thought they were entitled to go back twenty-two years. But they just make up the rules as they go along. It reminds me of George Ade's story of the man who was in prison and a friend went to see him and asked what he had done. The man told him, and the friend said, "But they can't put you in prison for that." "I know they can't," said the man, "but they have."

This letter ought to reach you quickly, as Irene Ward, the MP, is taking it over to England with her tomorrow.

78 Avenue Paul Doumer
Paris
April 22, 1945

Dear Bill,

This is now my official address. By a miracle we have been able to get a furnished apartment and we move in tomorrow. It is almost impossible to get an apartment in Paris at the moment, so you can imagine how thankful we are.

I'm sorry your short story didn't get over with the *S.E.P.* just because it was a war story. Odd that they should be so against war stories, it's a complete change of policy since the last number I read, which wasn't so long ago. At that time the synopsis of a *Post* serial would be something like this: "Dwight van Rensaeller, a young American officer in the F.G.I., has fallen in love with a mysterious veiled woman diffusing an exotic scent who turns out to be Irma Kraus, assistant Gauleiter of the Gestapo, who is in New York disguised as a Flight Lieutenant of the R.A.F. in order to secure the plans of the F.B.O. One night at a meeting of the I.T.D. he makes the acquaintance of 'Spud' Murphy, in reality a Colonel in the T.H.B., who is posing as Hitler in the hope of getting a free lunch at a German restaurant on Eighty-fourth Street. They decide to merge the Y.F.S. with the P.X.Q., thus facilitating the secret operations of W.G.C. Go on from there."

I was sorry to hear that Wesley Stout had been eased out of the editorship of the *Post*, to be succeeded by someone of the ghastly

125

name of Ben Hibbs. I have no confidence in a man who calls himself Ben. Would the *Post* have flourished as it did if George Horace Lorimer had been Georgie Lorimer?

Before I forget. In one of your letters you asked me if I had ever read anything by Trollope. At that time I hadn't, but the other day, after reading in Edward Marsh's *A Number of People* that Barrie had been fascinated by a book of his called *Is He Popenjoy?*, I took it out of the American library (for which, by the way, thank God; it makes all the difference to life in Paris). I found it terribly slow at first, and then suddenly it gripped me, and now I am devouring it. It's rather like listening to somebody very long-winded telling you a story about real people. You put up with his long-windedness because the people are so interesting. The characters live in the most extraordinary way and you feel the whole thing is true.

I read Trollope's autobiography before the war and enjoyed it. But I still don't understand his methods of work. Did he sit down each morning and write fifteen hundred words, without an idea in his head at the start how the story was going to develop, or had he prepared a complete scenario? I can't believe that an intricate story like *Popenjoy* could have been written without careful planning. Of course, if he did plan the whole thing out first, there is nothing so very bizarre in the idea of writing so many hundred words of it each day. After all, it's more or less what one does oneself. One goes to one's desk each morning, no matter whether one feels bright or lethargic, and before one gets up a certain amount of stuff, generally about fifteen hundred words, has emerged. But to sit down before a blank sheet of paper without a notion of how the story is to proceed and just start writing seems to me impossible.

I have been meaning to send you a story a man told me some months ago. He was an ex-merchant-navy man, and during the war was in charge of various tough sea assignments. I only put down hurried notes, so I may have got the whole thing wrong, but this is what I think he said. He was told off to take his ship to somewhere off the east coast of England to recover forty tons of nickel which had been sunk in a torpedoed steamer, which was in such a position that you had to approach it through E-boat alley. Does that convey anything to you? It didn't to me, though I assumed it must mean some sort of channel where there was a big risk of being attacked by enemy E-boats. The sunken ship was four miles beyond E-boat alley.

My next note consists of the words "Three mines," so I suppose the fellow encountered three mines on his way. Now it gets a bit clearer. When the divers went down, they found on board the sunken ship a lot of unexploded bombs and also a number of cylinders of poison gas. This, of course, made the enterprise very perilous, and you could work it up and invent a lot of suspense. Anyway, the blowout is that after they had all been risking their lives for quite a long time, they were informed by the Admiralty that it was sorry they had been troubled, but they, the Admiralty, had just discovered that previous to the sinking of the ship the nickel had all been transshipped, so they needn't bother. Cheerio and thanks awfully, in fact, and we'll let you know next time we want you.

It seems to me that you could get a short story out of that on the lines of my Hollywood one, "The Castaways," where the entire personnel of the cast sweat their guts out, writing a picture based on a popular novel, and then the studio discovers that it doesn't own the movie rights to the novel. How about it? Do you think you can do anything with it?

78 Avenue Paul Doumer
Paris
September 13, 1945

Dear Bill,

Life continues very pleasant here. It was a blow when they started rationing bread again, but I suppose they had to. Some sort of trouble is going on now between the wholesale and retail butchers, which has resulted in no meat for the populace for about two weeks, but something always seems to turn up. There is a mysterious Arab gentleman who calls on us from time to time with offerings. He has just come and fixed us up with a rabbit. Also a Dane (a stranger to me, but a reader of my books) has sent me an enormous parcel from Copenhagen, the only catch being that all the contents are labeled in Danish, so we don't know what they are. There are three large cans which I hold contain bacon, but Ethel, who is in pessimistic mood today, says they are floor polish. But surely even the most erratic Dane wouldn't send hungry people floor polish. The only way I can think of solving the mystery is to ring up a Danish friend of ours at Neuilly and spell the labels over the phone to him and ask him to translate.

I see in the Paris *Daily Mail* this morning that E. Phillips Oppenheim has managed to get back to his home in Guernsey by getting a lift on a yacht. He is seventy-nine, but must still be pretty fit if he can dash about like that.

I have always been devoted to Oppy. I saw a lot of him when we were living on the Riviera. I remember him coming to lunch one day not long after he had had a slight sunstroke, and he was taking no chances of getting another one. There was a big tree on the terrace, through the leaves of which no ray of sunlight could penetrate, and he sat under it all the afternoon with a solar topee on his head, holding up an enormous umbrella, so he scraped through all right that time.

Did you know that he always dictated his books? I found him in gloomy mood one day. He had had the perfect secretary, who used to squeal with excitement as the story got going on the international spies and mysterious veiled women, which bucked him up enormously, and she had left to get married and in her place had come one of those tall, statuesque, frozen-faced secs whose idea of light reading is Kant's *Critique of Pure Reason*, and she took dictation in an aloof, revolted sort of way, as if the words soiled the paper of her notebook. He said it discouraged him.

How anybody can compose a story by word of mouth face to face with a bored-looking secretary is more than I can imagine. Yet Oppy thought nothing of saying, "Ready, Miss Spelvin? Take dictation. Quote No comma Sir Jasper Murgatroyd close quotes comma said no better make it hissed Evangeline comma quote I would not marry you if you were the last man on earth period close quotes. Quote Well comma I'm not comma so the point does not arise comma close quotes replied Sir Jasper comma twirling his mustache cynically period. And so the long day wore on period. End of chapter."

If I had to do that sort of thing, I should be feeling all the time that the girl was saying to herself as she took it down, "Well comma this beats me period. How comma with homes for the feebleminded touting for custom on every side comma has a moron like this Wodehouse succeeded in remaining at large as of even date mark of interrogation."

The nearest I ever got to it was when Ethel bought me one of those machines Edgar Wallace used to use, where you talk on to a wax cylinder and then turn back to the beginning to hear how it has come out. I started *Thank You, Jeeves* on it, and when I played it back I was appalled how unfunny the stuff sounded. I hadn't known it till then, but apparently I have a voice like a very pompous clergyman intoning. Either that or the instrument was pulling my leg. It stunned me. I had been hoping, if all went well, to make *Thank You, Jeeves* an amusing book—gay, if you see what I mean—rollicking, if you still follow me, and debonair, and it was plain to me that a man with a voice like that could never come within several million light-miles of being gay and debonair. With him at the controls, the thing would develop into one of those dim tragedies of the gray underworld which you return to the library after a quick glance at the first page. I sold the machine next day, and felt like the Ancient Mariner when he got rid of the albatross.

I don't know what we shall do this winter, but I imagine we shall take on the apartment for another three months and dig in. We have laid in a supply of wood big enough to last us through the cold weather, and things seem much better as regards electricity, so that we shall have electric stoves. Last winter was awful. The electricity wasn't turned on till five in the afternoon, and some days not before nine. I shall never forget a dinner given to us by a friend in a mysterious restaurant somewhere near here. We dined in pitch darkness and there were three black poodles in the room, so that every time anyone moved they stepped on them, and dinner was punctuated with agonized yelps.

36 Boulevard Suchet
Paris (16)
November 9, 1945

Dear Bill,

Note the above address. We move out of this apartment in a day or two and go to this other one, a very ornate joint belonging to Lady Deterding, two doors off the Duke of Windsor. I think we shall be very comfortable. About the only drawback to the place is that it is rather a long way from the shops, and, of course, everything has to be fetched—by me. By the way, the relief of having got rid of bread tickets is tremendous. I have always been O. C. Bread, going out in the morning before breakfast for it and being responsible for seeing that the tickets lasted out, and it was always a very near thing and a great anxiety. One month I had to borrow a chunk from the concierge on the last day.

I was intending to write to you last night, but I wouldn't have had time to write a long letter, so I put it off till this morning, and at breakfast your letter of November 4 arrived. I'm so glad you managed to fix up the novel so that it did not clash with H. M. Tomlinson's, but what a lot of bother you have had about it and all unnecessary really. I don't think there was ever a chance that Tomlinson would have made a fuss. With the great number of novels published nowadays, writers are bound to clash in the way of ideas. Still, it's best, of course, to avoid any possible trouble, as you have done.

I'll tell you what makes life hell for writers, and that is that you meet someone who tells you a story as having happened to himself or a friend, and you work it up and publish it, only to find that the gentleman read the thing in a magazine somewhere. But listen. What is *plagiarism?* Did you ever see a play by Freddie Lonsdale called *The Last of Mrs. Cheyney?* It was about a society woman who was one of a band of crooks, and this is revealed to the audience at the end of Act I. An exactly similar situation was in an American play called *Cheating Cheaters.* And the big scene of Act Two was where the hero gets Mrs. Cheyney into his room at night and holds her up by saying he is going to keep her there till they are found in the morning, which is exactly the same as Pinero's *Gay Lord Quex.* And yet nobody has ever breathed a word against Freddie for plagiarizing. Quite rightly. The treatment is everything.

I had to break off at this point to take Ethel's Peke Wonder for her walk. I find it almost impossible to get anything done in the mornings, as I have to suit my time to hers. What I would like would be to hoick her out of bed at eight-thirty, exercise her, and be able to settle down to work at ten. But if I try to do this, she curses so much that I desist. It is generally about eleven-fifteen, when I am just getting going, that there is a thud on my door, and in she bounds. There is a spaniel who lives at No. 72 and sits inside the front door, which is of thick glass, and every day Wonder toddles up to this door and she and the spaniel start a terrific fight through the glass, which lasts until I haul her away. The other day the spaniel nipped away and suddenly appeared at the open ground-floor window, whereupon a scene of perfect camaraderie ensued, both dogs immediately becoming bosom friends. But next day the fight started again.

Back to the subject of plagiarism. The best plagiarism story I know was the one Guy Bolton told me about Owen Davis, the American playwright. He had a show on in New York, a melodrama, and a tailor claimed that it was stolen from a play which he —the tailor—had dashed off in the intervals of tailoring. Davis got together with him and asked him just what he based the accusation on. The tailor said his play was about a man accused of murder and all the time he was innocent, and so was Davis's. Davis then took him round to some of the other plays running on Broadway at the moment—*The Crimson Alibi, At 9:45, The Sign on the Door*, etc.—and pointed out that these too were about men accused of murder and, by golly, in the end they turn out not to have done it after all. But you can't down a tailor with evidence of that sort. "They've ALL stolen my play!" was his only comment.

Frank Sullivan wrote a very funny article at the time when a Miss Georges Lewis sued Eugene O'Neill, charging him with stealing *Strange Interlude* from a play of hers called *The Temple of Pallas Athene*. Asked for the examples of similarity between her play and his, she cited these:

> I have been sadly disillusioned. (Lewis)
> You have been sadly disillusioned? (O'Neill)
>
> My goodness. (Lewis)
> My goodness. (O'Neill)

"I shall sue O'Neill, too," Frank wrote. "And I may even sue Georges as well, because, strangely enough, in my play *The Forgotten Galosh*, there occurs not only the line 'He has been sadly disillusioned' but also the line 'My goodness.' This, to my mind, makes it look very very bad for Georges and Eugene. Even if great minds do jump, three of us would never have thought of that pearl. It looks fishy to me."

He ends:

"I have plenty more evidence, which I propose to produce at the proper time unless the playwrights mentioned above see fit to settle out of court. I'll take ten dollars.

"Well, five.

"Not a cent under three. I'd be losing money.

"Well, don't go, hold on a minute, I'll take a dollar.

"A half-dollar I'll take.

"Could you spare a nickel for a cup of coffee?"

Which is about how most of these plagiarism suits wind up.

Dear Bill,

The new apartment is a great success. It's like living in the country with all the advantages of town. We are right on the Bois, which of course is a heavenly place to be near. We have hot water all the time, and we can keep one room warm with wood fires, so we are well off. We have a female Pole who comes in each morning and fixes lunch. Ethel fires her on Mondays and Thursdays. On Tuesdays and Fridays she resigns on her own account. On Saturdays and Sundays she doesn't put in an appearance. So our big day is Wednesday. Then is the time to catch us.

Food is still expensive—butter six dollars a pound—but we have had so many parcels from America that we manage all right. My trouble is that the shortage of bread in the prison camp has left me with a yearning for the stuff, and the present rations are very small. We just get through the month. But what has become of the potato? I had always supposed that in times of food shortage you just lived on potatoes, but they are like jewelry in Paris.

I had a letter from someone the other day, drawing a very gloomy picture of the short story situation in England. He says there is practically no market, and if you do write a short story it mustn't be over 2,000 words. Bobbie Denby, writing from America, says that over there you mustn't exceed 3,500. If this is true, it dishes me completely, as I can't keep under 7,000. I always construct a short story in three acts, as it were—punch at the end of the first 1,500 words, another punch at about the 6,000 mark, and then the 1,000-word finish. So 3,500 words wouldn't give me any room. I should imagine that all the old *Saturday Evening Post* writers must have closed up shop, because most of them felt that they were being a bit abrupt if they didn't come through with 10,000 words.

I'm longing to see your book. Reading the two readers' reports, I got the impression that what they shook their heads over was the length. I mean to say, 215,000 words! At a time when they've probably only got about half a dozen bits of paper in the office. I may be able to suggest cuts. Did you read Kipling's autobiography? In that he maintains that the principal thing in writing is to cut. Somerset Maugham says the same. Kipling says it's like raking the slag out of a fire to make the fire burn brighter. I know what he means. You can skip as you read, but if the superfluous material is there, it affects you just the same. I generally find with my own things that it's unnecessary lines in the dialogue that are wrong.

I've just read Raymond Chandler's *Farewell, My Lovely*. It's good. But a thing I've never been able to understand is how the fictional private eye drinks so much and yet remains in the hardest physical condition. In one of Peter Cheyney's books the sleuth drank eleven highballs and, immediately on polishing off the eleventh, went out and beat up not just one sinister character but a whole gang of them. Do you read Rex Stout's Nero Wolfe and Archie Goodwin stories? A good many of them came out in the *Post*. They are terrific, and the best part of them is that Archie Goodwin sticks to milk.

You say you tend to get tired nowadays. Me, too. After all, we're both heading for seventy. Silver threads among the gold, laddie. Extract from a book I was reading the other day: "Latterly his mind had been going to seed rather. He was getting on toward seventy, you see." Have you ever noticed, by the way, what peculiar ideas writers have as to what constitutes old age? "He was a man not far from fifty, but still erect and able to cross the room under his own steam," they write. Or "Old though the Squire was, his forty-six years sat lightly upon him." At sixty-eight I have reached the stage when, picking up a novel and finding that a new character the author has introduced is sixty, I say to myself, "Ah, the young love interest."

Dear Bill,

Hooray! The French Government have now assured me officially and in writing that I am no longer a danger to the Republic. I never was, as a matter of fact. Actually, I was very fond of the Republic and wouldn't have laid a finger on it if you had brought it to me asleep on a chair, but they did not know this and I suppose you couldn't blame them for feeling nervous.

The document revealing this change of heart was brought to me by an *agent de police*—they aren't called *gendarmes* in Paris—but my pleasure in reading it was marred by the arrival shortly afterwards of a spectacled Frenchman with a bill for thirteen thousand francs for electricity, this including a nine thousand penalty for overindulgence during the winter. Ethel nearly fainted, and I, though a strong man, was shaken. I had always feared we were for it, as we went in freely for hot water and heating during the winter months, but I had supposed that they would just shake a playful finger at us and fine us a few bob. Still, it's better than being cold.

I started reading *Fool's Gold* last night and have just reached Page 136, and my opinion so far is that it is one of the most fascinating things I have ever read. The idea of cutting a line of it revolts me. And at the same time I am saying to myself, "Am I all wrong about this book? I mean, is my mind so constituted that I am the only person who would enjoy it?" Which, I gather from your letter, is exactly the impression it makes on you. You say, "I don't believe anyone would be interested in the book except myself."

I don't think you're right about that, but I do think its reception depends a good deal on what the reader is led to expect. If he thinks he is going to get a quick-moving, dramatic story of the Old West, then I suppose he might be disappointed, but I can't believe that anyone would find it uninteresting. Anyway, I like it.

Which reminds me of the story of the actress whose sister telegraphed her on the opening night of her new show, "Whatever happens, Mother and I love you."

I return the Rich and Cowan letter about your "coarseness," also the two readers' reports. I often wonder how a publisher ever accepts a novel on a reader's report. What bleak, barren productions they are. Typical reader's report of *Henry Fourth, Part One*, by W. Shakespeare: "This is a story of life in London, with very little to recommend it. The plot is improbable and does not carry conviction, as it deals with a Prince of Wales who visits saloons. There is a fat man named Falstaff."

I wouldn't worry about Rich and Cowan's letter. Why shouldn't you be coarse? You're writing about coarse people— sailors and tough characters generally—so let them be tough. The trend is all that way today. Ethel came back from a shopping binge yesterday bringing a book called *Night and the City* by Gerald Kersh. Do you know his work? I've seen his name about, but the only thing of his I had read was a short serial in *Collier's*. This book is terrific, and talk about coarseness! Sordid to a degree, with only one moderately decent character in it. An odd thing is that it was apparently published originally by Michael Joseph and is now issued by Heinemann. I should imagine that what happened was this. M. Joseph brought it out some years ago, sold about two thousand copies, and then called it a day, and the plates, or whatever they call them, returned to the author. Then there were six years of war, ending with a general coarsening of the public taste, and Heinemann felt that what was too sordid for readers in 1937 or whenever it was would now be just right for them. If you ask me, I think novels are going to get dirtier and dirtier, and in another ten years anything will go. So, if I were you, I'd carry on regardless.

Yes, I read in the Paris *Herald Tribune* about Jerry Kern's death, and it was a great shock to me. I was always very fond of him, and he was an angel to work with, which a good many composers weren't. I saw him very rarely after the road tour of *Sitting Pretty* in 1924. The last time we met was in Hollywood in 1936, and I remember thinking how frail he looked. He had a terrible time in the great stock market crash, losing one fortune in 1929 and another in 1931, and it had affected his heart.

We did nine shows together—or ten, if you count *Sally*, to which I contributed some lyrics. I believe he got rather solemn and serious toward the end of his life, but in the Princess Theatre days he was one of the most cheerful and amusing fellows I have ever met, always up to something crazy. I remember spending the weekend at his house in Bronxville once, and around midnight on the Saturday I happened to mention that Ethel and I had taken a bungalow at Bellport for the summer. "Let's go and look at it," said Jerry. "Tomorrow, you mean?" I said. "No, now," said Jerry, and he insisted on driving off there and then in his car.

Bronxville is about thirty miles one side of New York and Bellport about seventy miles the other side. We got there at three in the morning, inspected the bungalow, and drove back, Jerry at the wheel sound asleep most of the time. I had to keep nudging him, and he would wake up and say, "Oh, did I doze off? Sorry." It wasn't one of the rides I look back to as among my most enjoyable.

⤜⤛⤜

I first met Jerry Kern in the summer of 1906. I had a job at that time as a sort of bottle washer—a writer of extra lyrics, encore verses, etc., at the Aldwych Theatre in London, where Charles Frohman was putting on musical comedies starring Seymour Hicks. A new show was in preparation, and one night Hicks took me along to listen to some music by a young American composer. A promising young fellow, Hicks said Frohman said he was. His name, new to me, was Jerome Kern.

The word "young" was well chosen. Actually, Jerry was nineteen, but he looked about fifteen. He was very gay and cheerful, and so was what he played to us. Hicks bought three of his tunes and I fitted words to them. One of my lyrics was a shocking steal from "Mister Dooley" (called "Mister Chamberlain") and a pretty poor effort all around, but Jerry's melody was so terrific that the number used to get six or seven encores every night and was the big moment in the show.

It was not until 1914 that we met again, at the opening of *Very Good Eddie* at the Princess Theatre on Thirty-ninth Street, whither I had gone in my capacity of dramatic critic to *Vanity Fair*. He was with Guy Bolton, who had written the book, and he remembered our "Mister Chamberlain" so well that he suggested that he and Guy and I should team up. That was the start of what have become known as "the Princess shows," small intimate musical comedies with clever books by Guy, fascinating scores by Jerry, and—I hope—adequate lyrics by the undersigned.

The Princess shows brought Jerry fame and money, and nobody could say that he had not earned them. Even more than most composers he had had his early struggles, and though there is nothing much to be said in favor of early struggles while you are struggling, they do unquestionably turn their victim from an amateur into a professional. They give him the confidence that, if he has gone through all that, he can do anything. By the time Jerry achieved success, he was ready for it.

He had begun his career in the lower depths of Tin Pan Alley, playing his publishers' songs in a song plugger's cubicle, adapting foreign songs for the American market, making new arrangements of old songs, and plugging songs in department stores. From this he rose to getting a few numbers interpolated in an occasional musical by some more eminent composer, and from that to getting more numbers interpolated, and as these were nearly always the outstanding hits of the shows in which they appeared, he began to attract attention. "Who is this Jerome Kern whose music towers in an Eiffel way above the average primitive hurdy-gurdy accompaniment of the present-day musical comedy?" wrote one of the important New York critics.

It was the first World War that gave him his chance. The standard procedure with managers until it broke out had been to import Viennese operettas and try to brighten them with a couple of Kern numbers, and when war came it was no longer possible to import Viennese operettas. It became necessary to look about for American composers, and they did not have to look far before finding Kern. Ray Comstock of the Princess was the lucky man to find him first. Charles Dillingham came next, and then Ziegfeld. In 1917 Jerry was sole composer of *Have a Heart, Love O' Mike, Oh Boy*, and *Leave It to Jane*, in 1918 of *Oh, Lady! Lady! Toot-Toot, Rock-a-Bye Baby*, and *Head over Heels*. There was no stopping him. His well of melody was inexhaustible, and he loved work. You could not give him too much of it.

It was this habit of always working and very seldom sleeping that undermined his health. He hated to go to bed. His idea of a quiet home evening was to sit at the piano, composing, till about five in the morning. Not once but several times in the Princess days my telephone would ring in the small hours.

"Plum? Jerry."

"Good heavens, Jerry. Do you know what time it is?"

This would puzzle him.

"Quite early, isn't it? Are you in bed?"

"I was."

"Oh? Well, I've just got that first act number we were worrying about. Get a pencil and paper."

His telephone was on the piano, and he would play me the melody and I would take down a dummy and totter back to bed. Jerry probably stayed up and worked on the second act trio.

Even a strong man could not do this sort of thing year after year without paying the penalty, and Jerry was always frail. He was what Kipling called "over-engined for his beam." Very suddenly he collapsed. On the morning of November 5, 1945, he was walking down Park Avenue on his way to a rehearsal and without any warning fell in mid-stride. He was taken to the Doctors Hospital but never regained consciousness. He died on November 11. In forty-one years he had written over a thousand songs and had composed the scores of thirty-six musical comedies and twenty motion pictures. Radio stations throughout the country held programs to honor his memory, and from Washington President Truman sent this telegram:

His melodies, surviving him, will live in our voices and warm our hearts for many years to come, for they are the kind of simple, honest songs that belong to no time or fashion.

He was right. Pure melody, like Jerry's, does not date.

P.G.W.

Pavillon Henri Quatre
St.-Germain-en-Laye
November 1, 1946

Dear Bill,

Lady Deterding wanted her apartment back, so we moved and came here. This is the spot to be. Nine miles out of Paris, but right in the country. This hotel is on the edge of a terrace a mile and a half long which looks all over Paris, and at the back of the terrace there is a forest. Trains to Paris every quarter of an hour do the journey in twenty-five minutes, landing you in the heart of the city, so that I am really just as near to the American Library as I was at the Boulevard Suchet. This is the house where Louis the Fourteenth was born, if that interests you.

I sent you a copy of *Joy in the Morning* yesterday. I hope you'll like it. I don't think it's bad, considering that most of it was written during the German occupation of Le Touquet, with German soldiers prowling about under my window, plus necessity of having to walk to Paris Plage every morning to report to a German Kommandant with a glass eye.

This matter of glass-eyed German Kommandants, by the way, is one that should be carefully gone into by the United Nations. One recognizes, of course, that in modern total warfare the innocent bystander can no longer consider himself immune from unpleasantness, but there are surely limits to what should be inflicted upon him. I used to amble down to Paris Plage of a morning like Pippa passing, and I would go in at the door of the Kommandatura and meet that eye and wilt. It was like the Boss's eye you read about in the advertisements, and everyone knows how hopeless it is to try to meet that without wilting unless you have subscribed to the correspondence course in character-building and self-confidence.

I had to fix up a couple of spots in *Joy in the Morning*. At one point Bertie spoke of himself as eating a steak, and Boko Fittleworth was described as having a fried egg for breakfast, and this agitated Grimsdick of Jenkins a good deal. He said that the British public is so touchy about food that any mention of steaks and eggs would cause an uproar. I cut out the steak and changed the egg to a sardine, so I hope all will now be well.

When you spoke enthusiastically of J. B. Priestley's book, did you mean *Bright Day?* I read that and liked it, but I haven't seen any others by him. I am now reading Evelyn Waugh's *Put Out More Flags* and am absolutely stunned by his brilliance. As a comic satiric writer he stands alone. That interview between Basil Seal and the Guards Colonel is simply marvelous. And what a masterpiece *Decline and Fall* was.

I have been having a spot of trouble with my eyes lately, and it was a comfort to read what you said in one of your letters about paying no attention to those floating specks. If they don't matter, that's fine. But now when I move my right eye a sort of black thing swings across it. If it's only a blood vessel, right ho; but I was brought up on *The Light That Failed* and suspect any funny business along those lines.

Incidentally, why do all these critics—George Orwell, for instance—assume that *The Light That Failed* was a flop and is recognized as such by the reading world? It certainly didn't flop in the sense of making no money, as it probably sold several hundred thousand in the original edition and was also serialized and made into a successful play. And if they mean that it's a failure because it doesn't grip you, they're simply talking through their hats. I suppose for today it is a bit mannered, and some of that he-man stuff is hard to take, but it's a darned good story, and if anybody says it isn't, those, as far as I'm concerned, are fighting words.

Do you ever read George Orwell, by the way? He's awfully good and a very nice chap. He's a friend of Malcolm Muggeridge and about a year ago came over to Paris and stood Ethel and me an excellent lunch at a place down by Les Halles (The Markets to you). He struck me as a terribly sad man. I didn't see him again after that, but we correspond regularly. In his latest he says he has bought a house twenty-six miles from anywhere, up in the north of Scotland.

I wonder if a book about my camp experiences would be any good. The trouble about books of that kind is that you never know whether what has seemed hilarious to you won't bore the general public cross-eyed. As, for instance, the camp beards. A lot of us grew them, though I held off it myself and went on shaving daily. What I felt was that there is surely enough sadness in life without going out of one's way to increase it by sprouting spade-shaped whiskers. The fellows who did become fungus fanciers looked about as repulsive as it is possible to look, and one felt a gentle pity for the German corporal whose duty it was to wake them in the morning. What a way to start one's day!

O'Brien, one of the sailors, had one of those long Assyrian numbers, falling like a cataract down his chest, and it gave me quite a start when at the beginning of the summer he suddenly shaved, revealing himself as a spruce young fellow in the early twenties. I had been looking on him all the time as about twenty years my senior, and only my natural breeding had kept me from addressing him as "Grandpop."

Is that the sort of thing to give the customers, or is it just one of those private jokes which are frightfully droll, only you wouldn't see how funny it was unless you had known the chap? Difficult to say, and maybe the prudent course is to let the thing alone and not stir it.

> *Pavillon Henri Quatre*
> *St.-Germain-en-Laye*
> *April 1, 1947*

Dear Bill,

Do you ever write a novel knowing that it will stand or fall by some chapter near the end? It's a most unpleasant feeling. I'm up against that in *The Mating Season*. It's fine as far as I've got— about two-thirds of the way—but unless I can make the village concert chapter funny, the thing will flop. I'm hoping for the best.

And now let us speak of parcels. As far as I can gather, the entire postal service of the world has gone cockeyed, though I may be wronging the rest of the world and the fault may lie entirely in France. If you sent me the script of your book last Saturday, why haven't I had it yet, today being Friday? And if Nelson Doubleday sent me a parcel on November 27, why did it reach me on February 10? And why hasn't another parcel from England got here at all? Can Duff Cooper be pinching parcels, *too*? I wouldn't put it past him.

Since I last wrote, things have been moving on the Low Wood front. We have decided to rebuild. We expect the French Government to chip in with something pretty good in the way of footing the bills, but we have to pay out first and then they pay us back. The catch is that the French Government is cagey. It says, "Oh, so you lost all your baths, did you? Well, OK, here are some to replace them." But whereas your baths were expensive jobs in pink and mauve and so on, the Government takes the line that a bath is a bath and will only pay for the cheapest available. Same with chairs. You lose your posh chair for which you paid a fortune, and they give you a kitchen chair, and when you kick, they say, "Well, it's a chair, isn't it?" (Or, more probably, "C'est une chaise, hein?") So we shall have to dig down and pay the difference if we want the good stuff. Still, it'll be worth it, to have a home again.

We have booked our passage to New York, but when we shall be sailing I don't know. Everything is so uncertain these days. Thank goodness my American income-tax trouble has been settled after dead silence on the part of the Tax Court since October 1945. I'm not sure if I told you, but what happened was that the tax people suddenly got the idea that I had not paid taxes for 1921-1924, if you can imagine it. They impounded all my money over there. The Court now decides that I did pay tax in the years mentioned (as, of course, I did, only naturally all records have been destroyed years ago). The net result is that I shall get a refund of about $20,000, and I am feeling frightfully rich. I find nowadays that any cash any Government allows one to keep nowadays is velvet. Anyway, my whole financial position in America has changed overnight, and instead of landing without a cent and having to make a quick touch from Doubleday or someone, I have become self-supporting. Great relief.

I will let you know my New York address. It will probably be the Plaza, at any rate to start with. The Plaza has the enormous advantage that it is just opposite the Park, so that airing Wonder (which is, after all, the most important thing in life) will be simple.

Dear Bill,

Well, we made it. Here I am in New York and still feeling a bit dizzy.

We had one of those rough voyages that the sailors in your books are always having on the western ocean, which seems unjust at this time of year. But the worst part was before we started. We arrived at Cherbourg and got on the tender and then had a five-hour wait before the "America" showed up, it having been delayed by fog in the Channel. I've never felt so hungry in my life, not even at the Citadel of Huy. We just sat there hour after hour, with our stomachs sending up frantic inquiries to the front office, wanting to know what was happening. We finally got aboard at ten P.M. and had a belated dinner, which was worth waiting for. The caviar simply slid down.

It's just ten years since I was in New York. It's quite a business arriving there now. In the old days the only newspaperman one saw was the ship reporter of the N. Y. *Times,* who sauntered up as one was seeing one's stuff through the Customs and asked if one had had a pleasant voyage; but now a whole bevy of the gentlemen of the Press flock aboard at Quarantine and a steward comes to you and tells you that they are in the saloon and request your presence. It's like being summoned before a Senate Committee.

I found the reporters very pleasant, especially the man from *P. M.,* one of the evening papers. We became inseparable, and last Monday he gave a dinner for Ethel and me at his house down in Greenwich Village, where my evening was made by meeting Frank Sullivan. I have always loved his stuff, and he's a jewel of the first water.

My second morning I held a formal "Press Conference" at the Doubleday offices; the next day I was interviewed on the radio and the day after that on television. All this sounds as if I were no small potatoes and a hell of a celebrity, but the explanation is that Doubleday's publicity hound arranges it all in the hope that it will lead to the sale of a copy or two of *Joy in the Morning*. I don't suppose it helps a bit, really. I don't imagine the great public sits listening spellbound while I answer questions from the interlocutor and says, "My God! So that's Wodehouse! How intelligent he looks! What lustrous eyes and what a noble brow! I certainly mustn't miss that last book of his!" Much more probably they reach out and twiddle the knob and get another station.

Guy Bolton tells me that *Sally* is going to be revived with lyrics by me extracted from other Bolton-Wodehouse-Kern shows, and Gilbert Miller is reviving *The Play's the Thing* with Louis Calhern in the Holbrook Blinn part, but apart from that I don't think there's much chance of theatrical work. The whole situation has altered completely since I was here last. There don't seem to be any regular managers now, the sort who used to put on their three or four shows every season. Everything has become much too expensive, and today what happens is that some complete novice decides that he would like to have a pop, and he gets hold of a play and then passes the hat around in the hope of raising enough money to produce it. Though how anybody does raise the money beats me, for today you need a minimum of $50,000 for a straight play with only one set and for a musical anything from $250,000 up. Of course, if you have a colossal smash like *Oklahoma!*, it doesn't take you long to get your money back at six or seven dollars per ticket, but with an only fairly successful show the going is rough.

Irving Caesar, a pal of mine, put up some money for a musical that's running now, and he showed me the week's balance sheet the other day. The gross box-office receipts were $36,442.90 and the profit on the week was only $3,697.83, which means that they will have to go on doing nearly $37,000 a week for about seventy weeks before they can start making a cent. In 1916, with *Miss Springtime* at the New Amsterdam, we sold out regularly for a year at a weekly $16,000 and made a fat profit. At least, Abe Erlanger, who put it on, always looked well fed. Shows how things have altered.

❦

The man who interviewed me on television asked me among other things to describe my literary methods, and I did, but as listeners from coast to coast probably switched to another channel the moment I appeared on the screen, it seems the kindly thing to do to tell them what they missed. Here, briefly, are the facts.

I would like to say, as I have known other authors to say, that I am at my desk every morning at nine sharp, but something tells me I could never get away with it. The public is shrewd, and it knows that no author is ever at his desk at nine. I do get to my desk, however, around about ten-thirty, and everything depends then on whether or not I put my feet up on it. If I do, I instantly fall into a reverie or coma, musing on ships and shoes and sealing wax and cabbages and kings, with possibly a side-glance at the mystery of the Universe. This goes on for some time. Many of my deepest thoughts have come to me when I had my feet up on the desk, but I have never been able to fit one of them into any novel I have been writing.

If I avoid this snare, I pull chair up to typewriter, adjust the dachshund which is lying on my lap, chirrup to the Boxer, throw a passing pleasantry to the cat, and pitch in.

All the animal members of the household take a great interest in my literary work, and it is rare for me to begin the proceedings without a quorum. I sometimes think I could concentrate better in solitude, and I wish particularly that the cat would give me a word of warning before jumping on the back of my neck as I sit trying to find the mot juste, but if I gave them the bum's rush, it would simply mean that they would come scratching at the door or, in the case of the cat, mewing on the windowsill. Impossible, as I see it, to beat the game.

My writing, if and when I get down to it, is a combination of longhand and typing. I generally rough out a paragraph or a piece of dialogue or occasionally a page or two in pencil on a pad and then type an improved version. This always answers well unless while using the pad I put my feet up on the desk, for then comes the reverie of which I was speaking and the mind drifts off to other things.

I am fortunate as a writer in not being dependent on my surroundings. Some authors, I understand, can give of their best only if there is a vase of red roses—red, not yellow—on the exact right spot of their desk and away from their desk are unable to function. I have written quite happily on ocean liners during gales, with the typewriter falling into my lap at intervals, in hotel bedrooms, in woodsheds, in punts on lakes, in German internment camps, and in the *inspecteurs'* room at the Palais de Justice in Paris at the time when the French Republic suspected me of being a danger to it. I suppose it was the seven years when I was doing the "By the Way" column on the *Globe* that gave me the useful knack of being able to work under any conditions.

Writing my stories—or, at any rate, rewriting them—I enjoy. It is the thinking them out that makes the iron enter into the soul. You can't think out plots like mine without getting a suspicion from time to time that something has gone seriously wrong with the brain's two hemispheres and that broad band of transversely running fibers known as the corpus callosum. I always have to make about four hundred pages of notes before I can get my scenario set, and there is always a moment, as I read them over, when I pause and say to myself, "Oh, what a noble mind is here o'erthrown." I append a few specimens of my notes for the last one I wrote, *Service with a Smile.*

> *Father an actor? This might lead to something.*
> (There is no father in the story)
>
> *Make brother genial, like Bingo Little's bookie.*
> (There is no brother in the story)
>
> *Crook tells hero about son.*
> (There is no crook in the story. No son, either)
>
> *Can I work it that somebody—who?—has told her father that she is working as a cook?*
> (This must have meant something to me at the time, but the mists have risen and the vision has faded)

And finally a note which would certainly have aroused an alienist's worst suspicions. Coming in the middle of a page with no hint as to why it is there, it runs thus:

> *An excellent hair lotion may be made of stewed prunes and isinglass.*

The odd thing is that, just as I am feeling that I must get a proposer and seconder and have myself put up for Bloomingdale, something always clicks and the story straightens itself out. Very curious.

Hotel Adams
East 86 Street
New York
July 14, 1947

Dear Bill,

New York is simply incredible. About five times larger than when I last saw it. I said in a radio talk the other night that coming back was like meeting an old sweetheart and finding that she had put on a lot of weight. The prosperity stuns one after being in France so long. There is nothing you can't get here. And that brings me to a most important point. I want to start sending you food parcels, but before I do I must know what you're in most need of. I could put in a standing order with the British Food Parcels people, but the trouble with them is that they don't use their intelligence. When I was in France, I asked for tobacco, and they sent me a pound of it and a box of fifty cigars. Right. The happy ending, you would say. But mark the sequel. The following week another pound of tobacco and another box of fifty cigars arrived, and so on week after week, with the result that among my effects in storage in Paris are ten one-pound cans of tobacco and approximately a ton of cigars. So I don't want to go wrong with your parcels. Just write and tell me what you particularly need.

(I'm glad the flannel trousers arrived all right. Do you really mean to say they weren't long enough? They came up round my neck.)

The radio talk (see above) was with Mrs. Franklin D. Roosevelt, a charming woman, and I would have liked to have lolled back in my chair afterwards and had a long and interesting conversation about life in the White House. Unfortunately she threw me out on my ear the moment the thing was over—it was a taped talk due for release in two weeks—because John Steinbeck had

148

come in to do his interview. I think my performance was adequate. I wound up by telling that story about the woman who sat next to me at dinner and told me how much her family admired my work, my invariable procedure when interviewed on radio.

Why does one always say the wrong thing? Just to put him at his ease and to show him my heart was in the right place, I said to John Steinbeck, "And how is your play going, Mr. Steinbeck?", he having had one produced a day or two before. He gave me a long, wan, sad look and made no reply. I then remembered reading in the papers that it had come off after four performances.

⤸ ✠ ↶

The story which Plum mentions was of an old lady who sat next to him at dinner in London and raved about his work. She said that her sons had great masses of his books piled on their table and never missed reading each new one as it came out. "And when I tell them," she concluded, "that I have actually been sitting at dinner next to Edgar Wallace, I don't know what they will say."

W.T.

Hotel Adams
East 86 Street
New York
July 15, 1949

Dear Bill,

Yes, I agree with you about cutbacks. I never use them myself, but that's no argument against them. I am all for them in other people's books. I hate the type of novel which starts the lead character off in childhood, so that you don't get to the interesting stuff till about Page 124. There is something, too, about the cutback in itself which is valuable. It gives the reader a sort of double angle. I mean, he has become absorbed in the story of old Jones as a grown-up and then suddenly he gets a glimpse of him as a kid and the fact that he has been absorbed in him as a grown-up makes the kid stuff twice as vivid as it would have been if simply dished up as kid stuff at the start of the book. Not too clearly put, but you know what I mean. Denis Mackail works the thing in his new book, but there he does it in alternate chapters. He gives you a scene with his hero as of today, then the next chapter is back in the man's childhood, and so on all through. It's very effective.

I have sent you—at enormous expense, four dollars, no less—a book that has headed the American best-seller list for months, *The Naked and the Dead*. I can't give you a better idea of how the literary scene has changed since the old days than by submitting that novel to your notice. It's good, mind you—in fact, I found it absorbing—but isn't it extraordinary that you can print in a book nowadays stuff which when we were young would have been confined to fences and the walls of public lavatories? But whatever you think of the book, I'm sure it will interest you.

I have just received from the U. S. Treasury a donation of $4,500. What it is and why they sent it, I simply can't fathom. My lawyer says it's something to do with repaid interest on my 1941 tax. But the thing doesn't make sense. The Government put a lien on my money and won't let Doubleday's pay me what they owe me till the last of the cases is settled, and at the same time they send me these doubloons. The more I have to do with governments, the less I understand them. The result of my case before the Supreme Court isn't out yet, but I can't see why there should have been a case at all. The point at issue was, Does the money I got for *Saturday Evening Post* serials count as income? Any normal person would say, "Yes, of course it does; what else do you think it was?" But the Government is solemnly deliberating the point, and it is quite possible that they will refund me all the dough I paid in taxes on those serials.

❦

They didn't.

P.G.W.

Dear Bill,

Well, laddie, it's lucky I'm what George Orwell calls a wealthy parasite, for my chances of earning a living seem at the moment slim. Bobbie Denby was quite right—you do have to keep short stories down to 3,500 words; and how this is to be done baffles me. By the end of 3,500 words I'm just starting to flex my muscles and warm up. Furthermore, editors don't want stories with an English setting. And, still furthermore, they firmly bar what my agent Scott Meredith calls the "frame" story.

A frame story is the sort I have been writing for the past thirty years, where the thing begins with a group of people discussing some aspect of life and then Mr. Mulliner or the Oldest Member tells a story illustrating what they have been discussing. I don't know if this is clear, but take a thing like my "Strychnine in the Soup." That starts with a discussion of mystery novels and how shattering it is to be deprived of one when you are halfway through it, and then Mr. Mulliner tells about how this once happened to a nephew of his.

It has always seemed to me a good way of starting a story, because you can do your exposition amusingly and tell the reader exactly what the thing is about. But editors are against it, and they are the guys who call the shots.

If I ever do get going again over here, it will be entirely due to Scott Meredith. It's curious how we came to get together. He wrote me a letter when I was in Paris saying he liked my books, and we became regular correspondents. He was in the Army then, stationed at Fort Sumner, New Mexico.

He's an amazing chap. Only about twenty-five years old, but already one of the leading literary agents in New York. He started off as a writer at the age of fourteen, and by the time he was twenty had sold hundreds of things to the Post Scripts page of the *Saturday Evening Post,* as well as short stories and articles to other magazines. On coming out of the Army he got a job with a moribund literary agency which he and his brother subsequently bought with the bit of money they had been able to save. From then on he went steadily ahead, first with a tiny business and now with one that employs a whole squad of assistants. I don't know anyone I admire more. When I think how utterly incompetent I was at his age . . . ! I suppose the sort of life he has had develops one quickly. He told me that he was at a school in Brooklyn when he was a boy, the personnel of which seems to have been recruited from Devil's Island, and he had a fight with someone every day for four years. That kind of thing must toughen a chap!

Talking of fighting, there was an item in the N. Y. *Journal American* yesterday which brought back old times to me. Frank Graham, the *J-A's* sportswriter, wrote that Leach Cross, the boxer, was desperately hard up, and he appealed for contributions to help him along. I sent mine immediately. I had always admired Leach Cross. He fought as a lightweight against fellows like Jimmy Britt, Battling Nelson, and Ad Wolgast in the days when fights went forty-five rounds. He was never champion, but he came very near to it.

I met him in a saloon one night in 1904, when I had dashed over to New York for two weeks. I went over intending to go to the St. Louis Fair, but of course never got further than New York. I stayed with a man who had been a friend of mine in the bank— Nesbitt Kemp, a Californian who later became no end of a tycoon—and the odd thing is that I saw more of New York in those two weeks than in all the years I've spent there since. I believe the only way to see a city is to be a tourist. If you're a resident, you get into your own special groove, and if you're a writer, you're working so damned hard every day that you never have time to go anywhere. From 1909, when I settled in New York, until I married and went to live at Bellport, I was scarcely ever out of Greenwich Village, but in those three weeks in 1904 I was all over the place, making copious notes of everything, an industrious practice which got me chucked out of the celebrated Haymarket one night.

"These folks don't like you sketchin' 'em," the bouncer told me as he escorted me to the door. He wasn't angry, just disapproving.

I was terrifically keen on boxing in those days and had a boyish admiration for America's pugilists—Corbett, Jeffries, Kid McCoy, and the rest of them. I particularly wanted to meet Corbett, and I had a letter of introduction to him from an American in London, but he was in San Francisco when I landed and I didn't get to know him till many years later.

❧ ᴊᴄ ᴄ᷈

But I did meet Kid McCoy. I went out to the camp at White Plains where he was training for his fight with Philadelphia Jack O'Brien, and it was at the end of my afternoon there that I made what I can see now—in fact, I saw it almost immediately then—was a rash move. I asked him if I could put on the gloves and have a round with him. I thought it would be something to tell the boys back home—that I had sparred with Kid McCoy.

He assured me that he would be delighted, and we were preparing ourselves for the tourney when he suddenly chuckled. He had been reminded, he said, of an entertaining incident in his professional career when he was fighting a contender who had the misfortune to be stone deaf. It was not immediately that he became aware of the poor fellow's affliction, but when he did he acted promptly and shrewdly. As the third round entered its concluding states he stepped back a pace and pointed to his adversary's corner, to indicate to him that the bell had rung, which of course was not the case but far from it.

"Oh, thank you," said the adversary. "Thank you so much. Very civil of you." And he dropped his hands, whereupon Kid McCoy immediately knocked him out.

It was as my host concluded his narrative, laughing heartily at the amusing recollection, that, in Robert Benchley's powerful phrase, I developed a yellow streak which was plainly visible through my clothing. The shape of things to come suddenly took on a most ominous aspect.

"Is this wise, Wodehouse?" I asked myself. "Is it prudent to go getting yourself mixed up with a middleweight champion of the world whose sense of humor is so strongly marked and so what you might almost describe as warped? Is it not probable that a man with a mind like that will think it droll to knock your fat head off at the roots?"

153

Very probable indeed, I felt, and that yellow streak began to widen. I debated within myself the idea of calling the whole thing off and making a quick dash for the train. It was an attractive scheme, in which I could see no flaw except that the strategic rearward movement I was planning would put an awful dent in the pride of the Wodehouses. I had never gone much into the family history, but I assumed that my ancestors, like everybody else's, had done well at Crécy and Agincourt, and nobody likes to be a degenerate descendant. I was at a young man's crossroads.

At this moment, as I stood there, this way and that dividing the swift mind, as the fellow said, there was a clatter of horse's hooves and a girl came riding up. This was the Kid's current wife—he had six of them at one time and another—and she caused a welcome diversion. We all became very social, and the McCoy-Wodehouse bout was adjourned. I remember that girl as the prettiest girl I ever saw in my life. Or maybe she just looked good to me at the time.

It is curious, looking back, to think how informal training camps were in those days. No crowds of reporters, no throngs of spectators. As I remember it, we—the Kid, his trainer, a couple of sparring partners, and I—had the place to ourselves.

P.G.W.

1000 Park Avenue
New York
June 22, 1950

Dear Bill,

Note new address. We now have what the licentious New York clubman used to have in the silent pictures, a duplex Park Avenue penthouse apartment. There is a room on the ground floor where I work, and upstairs a living room and two bedrooms and a long gallery with French windows opening on a terrace which is about the size of a small English suburban garden. At the end of the terrace is a fence with a door in it, through which you get on the public roof of the building, invaluable for airing the dogs.

In addition to Wonder, we are now taking care of Guy Bolton's white Peke Squeaky while Guy is in England. She is a most lovable animal, very affectionate. Her way of expressing her affection is to scream like a lost soul, and when the Boltons were in Hollywood, the neighbors on each side reported them to the police, saying that they had a small dog which they were torturing. They said its cries were heartrending. So a cop came round to investigate, and Squeaky fortunately took a fancy to him and started screaming at the top of her voice, so all was well.

We have fitted the terrace up with a big hedge, trees, geraniums, etc., and it looks wonderful. We have all our meals there, and at night I sit out there and read. We are very lucky in that there are no high buildings within two blocks, so we get a fine view of the park and perfect quiet. We are on the thirteenth floor, and at night we don't hear a sound. I never want to go away from the place, even in the summer. We are only two blocks away from the best part of Central Park, where the reservoir is, and it's almost like being in the country.

The magazine situation is improving quite a good deal. *Collier's* took my last novel as a serial, and Scott Meredith sold a couple of my short stories to the *Cosmopolitan.* Not too bad considering that it is ten years since I had anything in an American magazine and only a few old buffers with long memories know that I ever was a writer.

The *Cosmopolitan* editor took me out to lunch and told me how much he liked my stuff and how he was counting on me for regular contributions, and I realized that I was breaking bread with what the young writer is always on the lookout for, the editor-who-believes-in-him. It was past three when he said he must be getting back to the office. When he did get back, he found on his desk an envelope containing the news that he had been fired. So all the weary work to be done again.

But how peculiar editors are. I met one at a cocktail party the other day, and he asked me if I had any short stories that would suit him. I said I had a couple lying around, and I sent them to him next morning. He accepted them with enthusiasm, and it then turned out that Scott Meredith had offered them to him a month previously and he had refused them. They were the same stories —not a word changed—so how do you explain it?

Story in the paper this morning. Wealthy-looking woman in mink coat gets on a Fifth Avenue bus and looks about her amusedly. "Goodness!" she says to the conductor as she gives him her fare. "It does seem strange to be riding on a bus instead of in my car. I haven't ridden on a bus in two years." "You don't know how we missed you," the conductor assured her.

1000 Park Avenue
New York
December 12, 1951

Dear Bill,

Sad bit of news in the *Herald Tribune* this morning.

FAMED BRITISH MAGAZINE
GOES OUT OF BUSINESS

is the headline, and it goes on to say that the final number of the *Strand* will be published next month. As practically everything I have written since 1905 appeared in the *Strand*, I drop a silent tear, but I can't say I'm much surprised, for anything sicker than the little midget it had shrunk to I never saw. And in my opinion never anything worth reading in it, either, the last year or two.

How on earth does a young writer of light fiction get going in England these days? When I was breaking in, I might get turned down by the *Strand* and *Pearson's*, but there was always the hope of landing with *Nash's* the *Story-teller*, the *London*, the *Royal*, the *Red*, the *Yellow*, *Cassell's*, the *New*, the *Novel*, the *Grand*, the *Pall Mall*, and the *Windsor*, not to mention *Blackwood*, *Cornhill*, *Chambers's*, and probably about a dozen more I've forgotten. I was looking at the book of acceptances and payments which I kept for the first five years of my literary career, and I note that in July 1901 I sold a short story to something called the *Universal and Ludgate* Magazine and got a guinea for it. Where nowadays can the eager beginner pick up one pound one shilling like that?

People wag their heads and tell you that what killed the English magazine was the competition of movies, motors, radio, television, and so on, but, dash it, these things are not unknown in America, and American magazines still go merrily along with circulations of four and five million. My view is that the English magazine died of "names" and what Scott Meredith, in his book *Writing to Sell*, calls slanting. I must send you a copy of that book, by the way. It's really excellent. I have always looked on myself as a hardened old pro who knew every move in the game, but I've learned a lot from it which had escaped me until I read it.

The slanter, for your information, is a bird who studies what editors want. He reads the magazines carefully and slings in a story as like the stories they are publishing as he can manage without actual plagiarism. And the editors say "Fine!" and accept the things, with the result that after a while the public begin to find the magazine's contents a bit like something they've read before somewhere and stop buying.

Names, though, were almost as deadly a poison. The *Strand* was better than most of them, but practically every English magazine would buy any sort of tripe, provided it was by somebody with a name as a novelist. The reason the *Post* was always so darned good was that it never fell into this trap. Have you read *George Horace Lorimer and the Saturday Evening Post* by a man named John Tebbel? Probably not, as I don't think it has been published in England. But here's what Tebbel says on Page 141.

> No writer was bigger than the *Post*. If one chose to leave, there were always others to succeed him. Nor could he give any less than his best for the *Post*, because Lorimer would not hesitate to turn down the work of the highest-paid writers if he thought it fell below standard. He read every contribution as though it were the first piece the writer had submitted.

That's absolutely true. Mary Roberts Rinehart in her autobiography says, "I once saw him turn down some stories by Rudyard Kipling, with the brief comment 'Not good enough.'" And Ben Ames Williams sold a hundred and sixty-two stories to the *Post* between 1917 and 1936, but several of his things were rejected during that time. The Boss was an autocrat, but, my God, what an editor to work for. He made you give of your best, all right. I had twenty-one serials in the *Post*, but I never felt safe till I got the cable saying each had got over with Lorimer.

1000 Park Avenue
New York
December 24, 1951

Dear Bill,

I returned a week ago from Niagara Falls, where I crossed to the Canadian side, spent a couple of nights, and came back into the U.S.A. as a resident, thus stabilizing my position and avoiding having to get renewals of my visitor's visa. I shall now be able to apply for citizenship, which has always been my life's ambition.

What a business it is doing this going out in order to come in again. I had to make three trips to Ellis Island, and I had to be there at nine in the morning, which meant that I woke myself up in the small hours and stayed awake so as not to be late. The boats to Ellis Island run every hour. If you miss the return boat, you have to wait for another hour, and I always did miss it by a minute. And nowhere to go except the corridor and nothing to do except pace up and down it. If I never see Ellis Island again, it will be all right with me.

I also had to have X rays done of my chest. I took them home and stored them in the archives, and on arrival at the American Consul's at Niagara Falls found that I ought to have brought them with me and couldn't get my visa without them. Fortunately the Consul had a heart of gold and let me wire to the Ellis Island doctor, asking him to wire back that my chest was up to sampler. When the doc's wire arrived, saying that it was the talk of New York and had five stars in Baedeker, I was given my visa. Next day the Consul drove me in his car to Buffalo, which saved me some tedious railroad traveling, and I am now back on the quota, so unless I plot to upset the Government by violence—which I doubt if I shall do; you know how busy one is—I can't be taken by the seat of the trousers and slung out.

But gosh, what a lot of red tape, as the man said when they tried him for murdering his wife. Very different from the old days, when I would be strolling along Piccadilly on a Tuesday morning and suddenly say to myself, "I think I'll go to America," and at noon on the Wednesday I would be on the boat en route for New York. No passports, no visas, nothing. Just like that.

Two interesting lunches this week. The first was with Michael Arlen, who, if you'll believe me, hasn't written a line in the last fifteen years. How he fills in his time, I can't imagine. The other was with Molnár, if you could call it having lunch with Molnár. When I arrived at one o'clock at the little Italian restaurant on Fifty-eighth Street where he had told me to meet him, he was there all right, but he had done his stoking-up at eleven, so I tucked in by myself with him looking on and encouraging me with word and gesture.

I always feel sorry for Molnár. What he wants is the café life of prewar Budapest, and I can see he is miserable in New York. He is homesick all the time, and nothing to be done about it. Also, the managers look on him as a back number and won't do his plays. I have adapted two of them—*Arthur* and *A Game of Hearts*—but I don't think there's an earthly chance of them being put on. *Arthur* has a different (and elaborate) set for each of the three acts, and the cost of producing it would be prohibitive. You would need about fifty-seven stagehands.

For the last few years he has lived at the Plaza Hotel on Fifty-ninth Street, and he never moves off the block where the Plaza is. He goes to bed at nine, gets up at five, has a cup of coffee, and writes till eleven, when he toddles around to this Italian restaurant —never going off the sidewalk, which runs across to Sixth Avenue and down to Fifty-eighth—has his lunch and then—around about noon—toddles back and is in for the night. Central Park is just across from the Plaza, but he never sets foot inside it. As I say, he doesn't move off the sidewalk—ever. An old friend of his from Budapest had trouble with his wife the other day, and as it was in all the papers and he knew Molnár must have heard about it, he was hurt that Molnár didn't come to see him and console him and wrote him a stiff letter, reproaching him. "My dear fellow," Molnár wrote back, "I am a very nervous man. I fear this New York traffic. You cannot expect me to risk my life driving through it in a cab every time your wife deceives you."

Well, there's one thing to be said for being in the New York theater world—you meet such interesting people.

1000 Park Avenue
New York
January 7, 1952

Dear Bill,

Your California book sounds as if it would be good. You were out there long enough to have absorbed quarts of atmosphere, and a book about life in Chula Vista fifty years ago ought to have an appeal. I remember those movie stories you mention. They were by Charles E. Van Loan, a very nice fellow who lost his right arm and taught himself to play golf with his left so well that he used to go around in the seventies with one arm. They came out in the *Post* and were published in book form by George Doran. The book was called *Buck Parvin and the Movies*. You might be able to get a copy from Doubleday, but after all this while I should say they were out of print. I should love to read them again. Isn't it amazing to think that in 1910 the movies were as primitive as that? As I remember Van Loan's book, you just got a camera and a few pals and went out into the desert and shot some pictures and that was all.

I wish you could get more publicity, though I am never quite certain how much publicity matters to an author. You have never done anything except write. Has this hurt you in competition with all those birds who never miss a literary cocktail party and go about lecturing and presenting prizes at girls' schools? It's hard to say. There's no doubt that the writers who shove themselves forward and suck up to the critics and tell interviewers what their favorite breakfast cereal is do catch the public eye more than recluses like you and me, who simply want to be left alone to do the daily chore. I always think that two-thirds of Hugh Walpole's reputation was the result of publicity. You couldn't stop that boy endorsing books and speaking at lunches and being noticed among those present.

I can't remember if I ever told you about my chat with Hugh when I was at Oxford getting my D. Litt. I was staying with the Vice-Chancellor at Magdalen and he blew in and spent the day. It was just after Hilaire Belloc had said in a radio interview that I was the best living English writer. I should have thought anybody would have spotted that it was just a gag, the sort Belloc was always getting off, but it worried Hugh terribly. He said to me, "Did you see what Belloc said about you?" I said I had. "I wonder why he said that." "I wonder," I said. Long silence. "I can't imagine why he said that," said Hugh. I said I couldn't, either. Another long silence. "It seems such an extraordinary thing to say." "Most extraordinary." Long silence again. "Ah, well," said Hugh, having apparently found the solution, "the old man's getting very old."

We went for a walk in the afternoon, and he told me that when somebody wrote a stinker about some book of his, he cried for hours. Can you imagine getting all worked up about a bad notice? I always feel about the critics that there are bound to be plenty of them who don't like one's things and one just has to accept it. They don't get a sob out of me.

The trouble with critics is that some of them are good critics and some of them are bad critics. An author likes the former but not the latter. A typical instance of the bad critic is the one on an English provincial paper some years ago who put a large headline at the top of his review which ran:

WODEHOUSE IS A PAIN IN THE NECK

When my press clipping bureau sends me something like that, an icy look comes into my hard gray eyes and I mark my displeasure by not pasting it into my scrapbook. Let us forget this type of critic and turn to the rare souls who can spot a good thing when they see one—and, shining like a beacon among these, is the woman who said in her book column the other day that she considers Shakespeare "grossly materialistic and much overrated" and "greatly prefers P. G. Wodehouse."

Well, it is not for me to say whether she is right or not. One cannot arbitrate in these matters of taste. Shakspeare's stuff is different from mine, but that is not necessarily to say that it is inferior. There are passages in Shakespeare to which I would have been quite pleased to put my name. That "Tomorrow and tomorrow and tomorrow" thing. That one gets over the plate all right. I doubt, too, if I have ever done anything much better than Falstaff.

I suppose the fundamental distinction between Shakespeare and myself is one of treatment. We get our effects differently. Take the familiar farce situation of the man who suddenly discovers that something unpleasant is standing behind him. In *The Winter's Tale*, Act Three, Scene Three, here is how Shakespeare handles it.

> Farewell!
> The day frowns more and more: I never saw
> The heavens so dim by day. A savage clamour!
> Well may I get aboard! This is the chase:
> I am gone for ever.
> (Exit, pursued by a bear.)

I should have adopted a somewhat different approach. Thus:

> I gave the man one of my looks.
> "Touch of indigestion, Jeeves?"
> "No, sir."
> "Then why is your tummy rumbling?"
> "Pardon me, sir, the noise to which you allude does not emanate from my interior but from that of the animal that has just joined us."

"Animal? What animal?"

"A bear, sir. If you will turn your head, you will observe that a bear is standing in your immediate rear inspecting you in a somewhat menacing manner."

I pivoted the loaf. The honest fellow was perfectly correct. It was a bear. And not a small bear, either. One of the large economy size. Its eye was bleak, it gnashed a tooth or two, and I could see at a g. that it was going to be difficult to find a formula acceptable to all parties.

"Advise me, Jeeves," I yipped. "What do I do for the best?"

"I fancy it might be judicious for you to exit, sir."

No sooner said than d. I streaked for the horizon, closely followed by the dumb chum. And that, boys and girls, is how your grandfather clipped six seconds off the world's mile record.

Who can say which method is the superior?

1000 Park Avenue
New York
September 24, 1953

Dear Bill,

There was once a farmer in Maine, so I learn from sources close to him, whose wife was subject to fits, and he used to get very irritated because when she had them people would call him away from his work to go and minister to her, and when he reached the house he would find she was perfectly all right again. This went on for years. So one day he was busy plowing, and a neighbor shouted to him, "Go to the house quick, Joe; your wife's in a bad way." And this time, when he got to the house, he found her lying dead on the kitchen floor. "Well," he said, "that's more like it."

The reason I bring up Maine is that I've just been there, trying out a play on what they call the "strawhat circuit"—i.e., the summer resorts, most of which have theaters now. You go from spot to spot, playing a week at each. Skowhegan, Maine, where *Life with Father* opened, was our first port of call. We did our eight performances, and on the Saturday the management informed us that the run would be continued at Watkins Glen, N. Y. We would drive there in a couple of station wagons. The cast knew nothing of Watkins Glen; nor did I. "Somewhere near here?" we asked. "Oh, fairly adjacent," said the management. About six hundred and fifty miles, they thought. Or it might be seven hundred.

So on the Sunday morning we started off. We got up at five-thirty, stopped in Skowhegan for a bite of breakfast, and then off through New Hampshire, Vermont, and Massachusetts. It was a great moment when we crossed the Massachusetts border into New York State, because there we could get a drink, a thing barred elsewhere on Sundays. (In Maine, by the way, you may drink sitting down, but you mustn't drink standing up. If you are having a snifter and start to your feet to welcome an old college chum who has entered the bar, you must be careful you aren't holding your glass as you do so, because if you are, you're breaking the law and rendering yourself liable to fine and imprisonment. There are local laws like this scattered all over America. In San Francisco, for instance, you mustn't shoot jackrabbits from a streetcar, while in Pittsburgh it's illegal to sleep in a refrigerator, the one thing we all want to do on warm summer nights.)

So picture us, *mon vieux*, tooling on and on through the long day on a journey about the equivalent in England of starting at Land's End and finishing up somewhere near the Hebrides. I enjoy my little bit of motoring as a rule, but it's a pretty gruesome experience to realize, after you've gone three hundred miles, that you've scarcely scratched the surface, so to speak, and that there are still another four hundred to go. Even assuming, mind you, that there was such a place as Watkins Glen. We only had the management's word for it, and they might easily have made a mistake.

Years ago, when Ethel and I had a penthouse apartment on the twenty-second floor of an office building on East Forty-first Street, we became temporary host and hostess to an alley cat which I had found on the sidewalk resting up after what must have been the battle of the century. I took him in, and for a few days he was a docile and appreciative guest, seeming to have settled down to bourgeois respectability and to be contented with regular meals and a spacious roof for purposes of exercise. There, you would have said, was a cat that had dug in for the duration.

But all the while, it appeared, the old wild life had been calling to him, and one morning he nipped out of the door and headed for the open spaces. And, not having the intelligence to ring for the elevator, he started to walk downstairs.

I stood above him and watched him with a heavy heart, for I knew that he was asking for it and that remorse must inevitably ensue. And so it proved. For the first few floors he was all jauntiness, walking with an air and carrying his tail like a banner, and then suddenly I could see the thought strike him like a bullet that this was going to go on for ever and that he had got to hell and was being heavily penalized for not having been a better cat. He sat down and stared bleakly into an eternity of going on and on and arriving nowhere. If ever a cat regretted that he had not stayed put, this cat was that cat, and after three hundred miles in the station wagon I could understand just how he had felt.

Well, sir, it turned out that there really was a place called Watkins Glen, and we reached it at four in the morning. We stayed there a week, playing in the high school auditorium with an enormous basketball arena behind the stage. This rendered the show completely inaudible. We then went on to Bradford, a journey of two hundred and fifty miles, where we got a theater but ran into Old Home Week, with the entire population dancing in the streets and omitting to come anywhere near our little entertainment, with the result that we played to about eleven dollars on eight performances. The management then announced that on the Sunday we would be leaving for Chicago. "Isn't that rather far?" we asked. "Far?" said the management. "What do you mean, far? It's only about a thousand miles."

At this point I put the old foot down firmly. I said I wished them well and would follow their future career with considerable interest but I was going back to New York. Which I did. The unfortunate company went off in an airplane, and I never saw them again, for from Chicago they jumped to Easthampton, Long Island—twelve hundred miles—and when I motored to Easthampton the Friday before Labor Day, I found there wasn't a bed to be had in the place, so twenty minutes after arrival I motored back again.

I was told later that I hadn't missed much. Our leading man had laryngitis and was inaudible, and the principal comic character started drinking, became violent, wrecked the house where he was staying, and was taken off to the calaboose. The police let him out each night to play his part and on Saturday for the matinee and then took him back to the jug again. This discouraged the management so much that they bowed out and went off to try to forget. So unless I can find another management to put on the show—say one that was dropped on its head as a baby and is not too bright—it may be considered dead. I see now that the real trouble with it was the same that James Thurber found in a play of his when he analyzed it in a calm, critical spirit after the preliminary tryout.

"It had only one fault," he said; "it was kind of lousy."

1000 Park Avenue
New York
November 10, 1953

Dear Bill,

You ask me in your last what I meant in my last by a basketball arena. Basketball is a game played throughout America in schools and colleges between the football and baseball seasons. It sort of sneaked up on me, because not so long ago there wasn't any basketball, and then suddenly it was all over the place like crabgrass. At each end of the arena is a basket, perched high up on the wall, and the object of the game is to throw the ball into these. Obviously, then, the taller you are, the easier it is for you to basket the ball, and the various teams scour the country for human giraffes who can just walk up and drop it in. And now the gamblers have turned their attention to the game and basketball scandals are popping up all over the place.

John Lardner has an article about this in *Newsweek* this week.

"I would like to tell the story," he said, "of a basketball game that was not fixed, some years ago. It seems that there was a fellow who went out on the street and met a tall man. The fellow stuck $500 in the man's pocket, which he could just reach, and whispered hoarsely, through a megaphone:

" 'The spread tonight against Kansas City is eight points.'

" 'Oh, is it?' said the tall man politely. 'Well, so long,' and he went down to the railroad station, bought a ticket to Albany, settled in that city as part owner of a coal and ice business, and lived happily ever afterwards.

"Basketball would be wholly honest if more people worked like that, because it is the wrong way to fix a game. For textbook purposes, the principle might be stated thus: You cannot assume that every tall man you see is a basketball player. Some of them are chartered accountants, some are taxidermists, and some are wearing elevator shoes."

John Lardner is the son of Ring Lardner, the short story writer, one of the most formidable blokes I ever met. He was at least eight feet high, with a grim, poker face, like Buster Keaton's. When you spoke to him, he never uttered but just stood staring coldly over your head. I sometimes think he must have been the hero of a story I heard once. Late one night this fellow rang the bell of a neighbor's house, and the neighbor, donning bathrobe and slippers, went downstairs and let him in, and it was apparent to him right away that the visitor had recently been hoisting a few.

"Hello," said the householder. No answer. "What keeps you out so late?" No answer. "Have a drink?" No answer. "Have a cigar?" No answer.

The belated guest then sat down and stared at his host for two hours without saying a word, and the host finally went to sleep in his chair. He woke as dawn was breaking, to find his guest still sitting and staring at him. Finally the guest broke his long silence.

"Say, why the hell don't you go home and let a man go to bed?"
he said.

The only thing that makes me doubtful about it being Ring
Lardner is that final speech. I don't believe Ring ever said as many
words as that at one time in his life. John Lardner is quite different,
very genial and pleasant. I had lunch with him the other day and
was dying to ask him if his father had ever spoken to him, but
hadn't the nerve.

1000 Park Avenue
New York
April 7, 1955

Dear Bill,

Life in New York continues jolly, but it would be much
jollier if crime was not so rife. It's all the go here these days. The
liquor store a few blocks from where we are was looted a few
days ago, and last week Ethel was held up at a dressmaker's on
Madison Avenue. She was in the middle of being fitted when a
man came in brandishing a knife and asked for contributions. He
got eighteen dollars from her and disappeared into the void.

There is something a bit crude about an operation like that, and
one feels that the fellow must have been rather a bounder. Probably went to the wrong school or something. A man like Charles
Raynor of 21 West Eighty-ninth Street, who prefers finesse, would
have raised his eyebrows if he had heard of such uncouth carryings-
on. Charles is the practitioner who recently took $6,200 off James
Joyce.

James Joyce—no, not the one you're thinking of—this one is a
sailor who lives in Philadelphia and not long ago was awarded
damages for losing a leg while working on his ship. When he met
Charles Raynor in a bar, he had $21,000. This was speedily ad-
justed.

After a few civilities had been exchanged, Mr. Joyce told Mr.

Raynor what a lot of money he had. On learning that what he had was only $21,000, Mr. Raynor expressed surprise that he should appear so satisfied. Wouldn't he, he asked, like more? Why, yes, said Mr. Joyce, he was always in the market for a bit extra, but the problem was how to get it. He could, of course, lose another leg, but for some reason he shrank from that. He couldn't tell you why, he just shrank. Mr. Raynor then said that it was a lucky day for Mr. Joyce when they met. It appeared that he, Mr. Raynor, had a friend, a Mr. Spiller, who had invented a magic box that made ten-dollar bills. Was Mr. Joyce interested?

Yes, said Mr. Joyce, he was. Interested was just the word. It was of a box of precisely this nature that he had often dreamed while splicing the main brace and porting his helm as he roamed the seven seas. He went with Mr. Raynor to Mr. Spiller's residence, handed over a ten-dollar bill, it was inserted in the box, there was a buzzing sound, and out came the ten-dollar bill together with a second ten-dollar bill. With a brief inquiry as to how long this had been going on, Mr. Joyce parted with $6,200 for working expenses, and the moment they had got it the Messrs. Raynor and Spiller parted from him.

I think these two men will go far. Indeed, the police say they already have.

The methods of Betty Welsh, who is a gypsy, were somewhat more elaborate, though she worked on similar lines. Meeting Alice Barber, a dentist's receptionist, in the street, she gave her a sharp look, asked if she might feel her pulse, and, having done so, delivered the following diagnosis:

"Yes, as I suspected, you have stomach trouble. Go home, light nineteen candles, and come back to me with thirty dollars wrapped around an egg."

This seemed sound enough to Miss Barber. It was just the sort of thing, she felt, that any good Park Avenue doctor would have recommended. She followed the instructions to the letter, but it turned out that further treatment was required.

"No, not cured yet," said Miss Welsh. "Yours is a stubborn case.

We must try again. Go home, repeat the alphabet backwards— better do this twice—and meet me here with a bottle of water, three potatoes, and forty dollars."

But even this did not bring relief, and for a moment Miss Barber's medical adviser seemed nonplussed. Then she saw the way.

"Go to the jewelry store on Fiftieth Street and First Avenue," she said; "get five hundred dollars' worth of jewelry on credit and give it to me. That should do the trick."

Unfortunately, Miss Barber told a boyfriend about it, and the boyfriend decided to take a second opinion. He called in the cops, and when Miss Barber and Miss Welsh arrived at the jeweler's, who should be waiting on the doorstep but Police Lieutenant Walter O'Connor and two gentlemanly patrolmen.

Interviewed later by the lieutenant, Miss Barber said:

"I had indigestion, so I thought I would give it a try."

A word on the subject of writing. I believe the only way a writer can keep himself up to the mark is by examining each story quite coldly before he starts writing it and asking himself if it is all right *as a story*. I mean, once you go saying to yourself, "This is a pretty weak plot as it stands, but I'm such a hell of a writer that my magic touch will make it OK," you're sunk.

1000 Park Avenue
New York
October 4, 1955

Dear Bill,

That last thing you sent me made me purse my lips a little, not because I didn't think it was a good story, for it is, but because you've made the Scotch—Scottish—skipper of your tramp ship talk broad Scotch—Scottish—all the time. I know Scotchmen— Scotsmen—oh, hell, north Britons—do talk in an odd sort of way, but I always think dialect ought to be used very sparingly in a novel. It may be just a personal prejudice, but when I see . . . and I swear I did. I'm not just making this up. It's in a novel by George Macdonald called *David Elginbrod,* and why I should have been reading it is more than I can tell you, because the title alone ought to have warned me that I was coming up against something hot . . .

Where was I? Oh, yes. When I find my eye colliding with a speech like "Meg! Whaur are ye gaein' that get, like a wull shuttle? Come into the beuk," I close the volume gently and return it to its shelf. (Which in this case gave me very little opportunity of enjoying George Macdonald's effort, because those are the opening words of *David Elginbrod*, so I didn't get beyond the first paragraph.)

I wonder if other readers are as fussy about dialect as I am. I don't even like those cockney stories where "What?" is printed "Wot?"

Slang's different. I'm very fond of slang in books. It's the misspelling of ordinary words like "where" and "you" and "going" that trips up the eye as it flits over the page and gives you the momentary feeling that you've stubbed your toe on something.

I often think there ought to be a law prohibiting English authors from using American slang. They do try so darned hard. They won't get it into their heads that slang is a condiment, not a fluid, and so will never let an American character say anything straight. There was a Broadway chorus girl in my *Damsel in Distress* who said to the hero, when he was beefing about being fed up with show business (he being a composer): "It's funny about show business, the way one drifts into it and sticks, I mean. Take me. What I ought to have done was buy a gingham bonnet and milk cows." When Ian Hay dramatized the book, this came out as "I may be a Broadway Baby to look at, Georgie, and a hard-boiled little hoofer from the Great White Way, but I was really intended to wear a sunbonnet and be a village belle way back in the great open spaces. The big little hick, that's me." I used to plead with Ian to have a heart and tone it down a bit, but he wouldn't. That was how Broadway chorus girls talked, he said. I suppose I ought to have been thankful that he hadn't made her say, "Twenty-three, skiddoo!"

More about the Crime Wave. It has come as something of a

shock to New York motorists to learn that the money they have been depositing in parking meters throughout the city all these months has not gone into the pockets of the authorities (whom they love) but into those of a total stranger named Giuseppe Nancini. The thought that they have been supporting Giuseppe to the tune of about $150,000 a year and that while they have had to rub along on near beer and hamburgers he has been wading into champagne and caviar is a very bitter one.

When, a year or so ago, Giuseppe got fired from his job as a parking meter maintenance man, he shrewdly stuck like glue to his official key, guaranteed to open five hundred meters in the Third Avenue area, and with its aid he proceeded to clean up, doing a nice $2,000 a night business.

But there is a bad catch to this thing of robbing parking meters. Parking fees are paid in dimes, and while dimes are all right if you can take them or leave them alone, it is embarrassing to have 1,500,000 of them about the home, as Giuseppe had. If you pay all your bills in dimes, people begin to ask questions. No doubt it was when he bought a $20,000 house and slapped down 200,000 dimes on the house agent's desk that suspicions began to be aroused. At any rate, four detectives jumped on his spinal column last week as he staggered up Third Avenue with approximately 20,000 of these coins on his person, and it is very doubtful if he will be with us again much before 1960.

Remsenburg
Long Island, N.Y.
June 14, 1956

Dear Bill,

The above is where we have bought a house and plan to spend the spring and summer every year. It's a very pretty village eighty-five miles from New York. When writing, address the letter "Remsenburg, N.Y.," because it's one of those primitive hamlets where you don't have a postman but go and fetch your mail from the post office.

Guy Bolton has a house here, and Ethel and I were staying with him and Virginia, as Guy and I were writing a play together. While we were working, Ethel explored the neighborhood and came back to lunch one day to say that she had bought this house. It's at the end of what is picturesquely known as Basket Neck Lane and has about five acres of land which lead down through a wood to a very attractive creek. Unfortunately one can't swim in this creek, as it is full of houses. Which sounds peculiar, but what happened was that when the big hurricane hit Long Island some years ago it uprooted a lot of houses on the shore and blew them into the bay, whence they drifted into our creek and sank. So if I dived in, I would probably bump my head on a kitchen or a master bedroom. Anyway, it's too muddy for comfort, so I do my bathing at Westhampton Beach, about six miles away, where one gets the ocean.

Westhampton Beach is a popular summer resort, and people spend the season there till Labor Day and during their stay take on dogs and cats and when they leave abandon them, the devils. We have been here only a few months, but already a foxhound and two cats have turned up and been added to the strength. One of the cats walks with me to the post office every day. The other cat arrived one night when Ethel was putting bread in the birdhouses in the middle of a blizzard, appearing from nowhere and leaping on the back of her neck. When we took it in, it was starving and had to have about six square meals a day, and Ethel said it wouldn't eat like that if it wasn't going to have kittens, so we must keep feeding it up. So we shoveled food into it like stevedores loading a grain ship and some time later took it to the vet's in Riverhead to find out when the kittens might be expected. The vet said we must not budget on seeing them in the immediate future, because the cat was a Tom. Apparently the reason it had waded into the food like that was that it was fond of food.

We finished the play late in the spring, and Guy, who always likes to have something to occupy his time, is now writing two musicals. Weird collaborators keep turning up to confer with him. One of them used to be a taxi driver. He was always thinking of funny gags, and when one day Eddie Cantor happened to take his cab, he sprang a dozen of his best ones on him, and Cantor was so impressed that he engaged him as one of his official gag writers. Since then this chap—Eddie Davis, his name is—has never looked back. During the war he had an idea for a musical comedy, but was of course incapable of writing it by himself, so the management called Guy in and the thing ran two years. Eddie has the invaluable gift of being able to raise money. He belongs to some strange club in the heart of Broadway which is full of men who are eager to put money into a show. So they have collected the two or three hundred thousand they need for this one, and it now simply is a matter of waiting till they can get a satisfactory cast.

It's now more than forty years since Guy and I began working together on Broadway, during which time we have written twenty-three shows and met every freak that ever squeaked and gibbered along the Great White Way. A few years back we had the thought that our reminiscences of the New York theater might make an interesting book and we did *Bring On the Girls!* (Title, Guy's.) Did you ever come across it? It was mostly about America, but there was a lot of London stuff in it, so many of our things having been done in England.

1000 Park Avenue
New York
August 3, 1958

Dear Bill,

Up in N. Y. for a few days, then back to Remsenburg. We have now got twelve acres there, as we bought a lot more land soon after we took possession. The new land looks fine. It was all jungle originally, but we had it cleared, and it now is a park like that of an English country house. We have also enlarged the house, adding a new kitchen, two sun parlors, and doubling the size of the living room. So from now on if you care to address your letters "Squire Wodehouse," it will be all right with me. (By the way, a fan sent me a letter the other day from England, addressed to "P. G. Wodehouse, America," and it reached me all right, which I thought rather a compliment.)

I came up here to get our television set. Have you one? I didn't like television at first, but revel in it now, especially a daytime serial called *Love of Life*, written by a chap named Don Ettlinger, and the fights. I never miss *Love of Life*. It comes on at noon, so of course ruins my morning's work. I suppose many people would dismiss it contemptuously as a soap opera, but it's nothing of the sort; it's a work of art, excellent construction and dialogue, and I wish I could get ideas the way Ettlinger does.

The fights are superb. They have them every Friday, and you get a much better view of them than if you were in a ringside seat. The second Joe Louis-Jersey Joe Walcott fight cured Ethel and me of attending these binges in person. We bought a couple of seats for some enormous price and found they were a mile and a quarter away from the ring. (This was an open-air bout at the Yankee Stadium.)

Talking of fights, is there a short story for you in this thing I read in one of the papers the other day? It was very long, but I'll try to condense it.

College Inn, Chicago, the year Jack Johnson beat Jeffries. There was a gang of newspapermen who lunched at the College Inn every day, among them a fellow called Lou Housman who was going to Jeffries' training camp to report on his progress till the day of the fight. He said as he was leaving, "Don't any of you bet a dollar till you hear from me. As soon as I decide how the thing's going to go, I'll wire Billy Aaronson." Billy Aaronson was the headwaiter at the College Inn.

Well, Housman went off to the Jeffries camp, and a week later Aaronson suddenly dropped dead. A new man, Marcel, took on his job, and one night he came in with a telegram.

"I don't get this," he said. "I open all wires addressed to Billy Aaronson, because they keep coming to him from people who don't know he's dead. But this one is different."

He showed them the telegram. It ran:

Aaronson
College Inn
Sherman Hotel
Chicago
Black—Lou.

Well, of course the newspapermen knew that it meant that
Housman was sure Johnson was going to win, and they had complete faith in his judgment, so they went out and put their shirts
on Johnson. They also made up a pool and bet it for Aaronson's
widow. The fight came off. Johnson knocked Jeffries out. They
all cleaned up.

About now you've begun to get a lurking suspicion that my
brain must have softened, if I consider there's anything in a story
like this. But wait. Days went by. They knew Housman must be
back in Chicago, but nobody saw him. He didn't come to the
College Inn. And then, about two weeks later, one of them
bumped into him and he confessed.

"I hadn't the nerve to face you fellows," he said. "I was so
darned sure. I thought I knew it all. I shouldn't have dragged you
boys in with me."

"What do you mean?" his friend said. "We were all set to bet
on Jeffries when your wire switched us. We made a killing on Johnson."

"On Johnson? Didn't Aaronson explain?"

His friend told him of Aaronson's death and said that Marcel
had shown them the wire and they had bet accordingly.

Housman nearly swooned.

"When I said good-bye to Billy that night," he said, "I gave him
a code. I didn't want the telegraph office there to know my pick.
So we arranged that if I wired 'white,' it would mean Johnson
and 'black' would mean Jeffries. I didn't think Johnson had a
chance."

Can you do anything with that? Wouldn't O. Henry have
jumped at it!

Dear Bill,

We are now settled here permanently, having given up the Park Avenue apartment. We found that we were using it only for about four months in the year, and having to pay $6,000 for four months seemed to us a bit too expensive.

I thought at first it might be dull living in the country all the time, but it isn't. I enjoy every minute of it, even the winters. We get snowed up twice regularly every year, but all we have to do is phone a man in Westhampton Beach and he sends a bulldozer and clears the drive, and the gardener digs paths through the snow, so we get along fine.

The hurricanes aren't too good—the last one uprooted twenty of our trees, including one that missed the roof of the sun parlor by inches—but they don't happen every year, and we now have a gas stove and one of those gas cylinder things, so we can cook when the electricity goes off, as it always does. Our first hurricane caught us off base, and we were three days without light and water and no means of cooking what little food we had. I breakfasted on cake and warm whiskey and soda and washed in the birdbath in the garden.

These hurricanes get going in the fall, but even in summer we are not without excitements. At Hampton Bays, close to where I live, a two hundred and forty-pound seal has clocked in and suns itself on the dock there daily, refusing to move over for dockside fishermen and sneering when they try appeasement in the shape of a dead fish. Naturally this annoys the summer visitors. There is nothing more unpleasant for a holidaymaker who has been up a little late the night before and has gone down to the dock for a morning swim to correct a slight headache than to find himself confronted by a seal which, so my Long Island paper says, "barks at all who approach." The last thing you want, at a moment when even a fly stamping on the ceiling sounds to you like riveters at work, is to have to cope with a barking seal.

Christopher W. Coates, curator of the New York Aquarium, says that all you have to do is to get a plywood shield and advance resolutely on the creature and it will retreat discomfited. All right, Christopher, you try it. You will find plenty of summer visitors to hold your coat and wish you the best of luck.

Even if it's not seals, it's something else. A neighbor of mine, chap who lives at the bottom of Basket Neck Lane, was annoyed by an odd noise in his car, sort of scratching noise, it sounded like. It went on for days, and eventually it occurred to him to open the bonnet and look inside, and there was a small white kitten. It was a bit disheveled and cursing quite a good deal, but still a cat, and is now, I believe, doing well.

So you see I was right in saying that life in Remsenburg is never dull. Always something going on.

So glad your book has been taken. I wonder why they made you change the title. *Eve* sounds all right to me. I suppose they thought it wasn't impressive enough. I remember in 1907, when Seymour Hicks was trying to find a title for his next musical, meekly suggesting *Peggy* and getting thoroughly sat on. "My dear fellow," he said, "you can't possibly call a big musical comedy just by a girl's name." Almost immediately afterwards a big musical comedy called *Peggy* was produced at the Gaiety, to be followed over here by *Irene, Sally, Mary, Sunny*, and about a dozen more.

Glad, too, that your eyes are so good. I wish I could say the same of mine. I never understand what oculists mean when they talk technical language, but the one I've just been to says my eyes are "off" fifteen points or degrees or something, which I take it is not so hot. The score, then, to date is that I am deaf in the left ear, bald, subject to occasional mysterious giddy fits, and practically cockeyed. I suppose the moral is that I have simply got to realize that I am in the seventies. I had always looked on myself as a sort of iron man whom age could not touch, which was where I made my ruddy error, because I'm really a senile wreck, with about one and a half feet in the grave.

The giddy fits come on every five years or so. At least, it's not exactly giddiness. The scenery doesn't get blurred and jump about. It's just that I lose control of my legs, regaining same next day. My doctor can't explain them. He said, "Well, if you have any more, you'd better just *have* them." I said I would.

You ask me if we find it difficult to get domestic help in the country, miles away from anywhere. Well, we've had our ups and downs, but at the moment everything is fine. We have Lynn, a dear little Polish girl, who lives about a mile away, and to do the cooking a very nice colored woman who lives in Riverhead seven miles away. Now follow this closely, because it's scientific. We have given Lynn our second car, an old Ford, and Gracie comes in with the bus from Riverhead every morning. Lynn picks her up at the bus stop and drives her here, and at night Gracie's husband comes in his car and drives her home. It works splendidly. Gracie has a brother who is a professional chauffeur, so I can always get him to drive me to New York when I have to go there, which is about three times a year.

I went there the other day to lunch with an editor. Nothing came of the trip except that Gracie's brother pouched twenty-five dollars. The editor wanted me to do some articles for him. "What sort of articles?" "Any sort. Write just what you like, laddie; write just what you like. Whatever you write will be OK with us." So I wrote an article and sent it in and haven't heard a word about it since then, which was over a month ago, so I assume that it wasn't what they wanted. It's always been my experience that if an editor says "Write anything," he means anything except what you do write.

<hr>

I have been brooding a good deal of late on this writing game. Why is it that instead of getting easier as time goes on, it gets more difficult? And why, after having had a good deal of success, do I suffer from this infernal inferiority complex about my work? I remember when I was starting out and getting nothing but rejection slips I was not in the least discouraged. I had the most complete confidence in myself. I knew I was good. It is only in these later years that I have become dubious on this point. Today I am a mass of diffidence and I-wonder-if-this-is-going-to-be-all-right-ness, and I envy those tough, squarejawed authors, smoking pipes and talking out of the side of their mouths, who are perfectly confident, every time they start a new book, that it will be a masterpiece.

My own attitude, when I begin to write, is like that of the late Sammy, the bulldog, when he used to bring a decaying bone into the dining room at dinnertime.

"Will this one go?" he seemed to be saying as he eyed us anxiously. "Will my public consider this bone up to the standard of previous bones, or will there be a sense of disappointment and a feeling that Samuel is slipping?"

Well, as it happened, each of old Sam's bones was just as dynamic and authoritative as the last one, and he never had anything to fear at the bar of critical opinion, but with each new book of mine I have that uneasy feeling that this time I have picked a lemon in the garden of literature. Good thing, really, I suppose. Keeps me up on my toes and makes me write every sentence half a dozen times. My stuff may not be the sort of stuff that admits you to halls of fame, but I do work at it. When in due course Charon ferries me across the Styx and everyone is telling everyone else what a rotten writer I was, I hope at least one voice will be heard piping up, "But he did take trouble."

P.G.W.

Remsenburg
Long Island, N.Y.
October 22, 1960

Dear Bill,

I have been meaning to write you for a long time, but I kept getting swamped with letters from readers of my books, all of which have to be answered.

They do write about the most extraordinary things. One man wants me to sell an old Dutch painting for him, another has had a letter from Winston Churchill (typed)—"Sir Winston Churchill thanks you for your kind letter of congratulation"—and thinks I ought to be able to get some millionaire to buy it for $5,000. (He won't take less than that. Would be giving the thing away, he thinks.)

But the pick of the bunch is a gentleman from California. He says, "I happened to buy the *Cosmopolitan* and on one of the front pages I see a list of authors and artists and I said to myself 'Those guys could put it over and I have a hunch they will,' and your name is on the list and I'm writing you along with the others to send me your check for twenty-five hundred dollars and write on the check that it is for a one-thirtieth interest in the Kid Gold Mine and then after awhile I will send you a check for your share of a million or a letter of regret telling you that I have spent that money digging through the mountain and my hunch was a bum one, but anyway I expect your check."

That was one I didn't answer.

Thornton Wilder, the playwright, when he reached his sixtieth birthday a few years ago, announced that he was going to celebrate it by getting tough with that section of his public which he calls the lunatic fringe. This includes the schoolchildren of America who write to him:

> Dear Mr. Wilder.
> Our English teacher has told us to pick an American author to write about, and I've picked you. When did you first start writing poetry? Do you believe in God? My paper must be in by the 16th, so please reply at once.

Communications such as this he will put firmly in the incinerator. He will also resell to secondhand bookshops all books sent to him for autographing and burn all manuscripts, epic poems, suggestions for novels, and privately published works submitted to him and tear up letters which say, "I, too, was born in Aries. Together we can write the book that will open men's eyes to the regenerative forces that are trying to reach them." For it is this sort of thing that has been making Thornton wilder for years and years, and he feels that at sixty he is entitled to lead a new life.

I was telling you in a recent communiqué that life is never dull in Remsenburg, there being always something doing either in or near it, and in support of this statement I will advance the story of one of the locals whom I will call X. It goes to prove, what I have often felt, that while considerable skill is needed to drive an automobile, the really tricky thing is getting into the vehicle. It is a task which, with Mrs. X at the wheel, taxes the stoutest. One day last week Mr. X wanted his hair cut, so Mrs. X drove him to the barber's in Westhampton Beach and waited for him in the street.

In due course out came X, smelling of bay rum and looking terrific, and he was about to enter the car when it suddenly jerked backwards, knocking him for what is commonly known as a loop. Kindly hands picked him up and dusted him and had started to insert him in the tonneau when the car again jerked backwards. The first time he had flown through the air for a matter of ten feet or so. This time he did fifteen. When, as he made his third attempt to enter it, the car once more jerked backwards, causing him to lower all previous records by managing twenty feet, he decided to call it a day and go to the local hospital.

Returning home after a brief stay, he found his wife standing on one leg before the refrigerator. She was standing there on one leg because in trying to shut the door with her foot she had caught her big toe in the hole left by the missing handle.

Sorry you're having trouble over the new book because the action covers a great number of years and you find it hard to handle. I'm not surprised. That's one of the things I've never been able to do—carry on a story over a long time. In all my books the action takes place in a few days, and it's a great handicap not being able to spread it out. I always like books (to read) where the author takes plenty of time. Have you read Angus Wilson's *Anglo-Saxon Attitudes?* I liked it. But isn't it extraordinary how all these modern authors make a beeline for homosexualism? It seems the standard motive in every novel you read nowadays. Query— Could Kipling have drawn Dick Heldar and Torpenhow in *The Light that Failed* as he did without having everyone assume that they were queer? That bit where Torpenhow is getting attracted to Bessie Broke and Dick comes in and says gravely,

"Can I have a word with you, old man?" and then urges on him the deadly peril of getting mixed up with a girl would have only one interpretation for the modern reader.

I have just the same trouble as you about slowing up in my writing. Is this old age, or is it simply that one is more particular about what one puts down? I think it good now if I do two pages in a morning. One needs constant encouragement these days, and that is why it's such heaven being with Simon and Schuster. Peter Schwed, who handles my books there, is the answer to an author's prayer. Possibly because he's one of my greatest friends, or possibly just because he feels that that's his job, he takes a personal interest in my work. S and S produce other books beside mine, but Peter always manages somehow to give me the impression that I'm the only author on their list who really matters. It's pretty comforting when you think how many impersonal sausage machines there are, where an author just delivers a book and hears nothing more about it.

A thing we both should bear in mind is that we are long past the age when most writers pack up and retire. But I can't picture myself retiring, can you? What I find about my own stuff these days is that if I get a good idea I can write it up better than ever, but that good ideas are very scarce. Generally, when I get one, it turns out to be something I wrote back in 1930 or thereabouts.

But sometimes—when in somber mood—I wonder if I really am a writer. I mean, take that internment camp, for instance. I was cooped up for a year with thirteen hundred men of all trades and professions and nothing to do all day but talk to them and find out about their jobs, and I didn't bring a single thing away with me. You in a similar position would have collected material enough for twenty novels.

There is this, of course, to be said in excuse for me—that it takes a steam drill to extract anything of interest from anyone. I tried to get some inside stuff from a man who ran a hotel in Boulogne—just my dish, I thought—and all he could tell me was that sometimes a customer asked him to have a drink. You can't make a powerful 80,000-word novel out of that.

I met a woman the other day whom I used to know back in 1912 or thereabouts, and she said, "I don't like your books. Why don't you write about *real* things?" "Such as?" I asked. "Well, my life, for instance." "Tell me all about your life," I said, thinking that this was it at last. And she mused for a while and came up with the hot news that when in Singapore during the war she had gone around with a tin helmet on her head. I tried to explain to her that that would be terrific for—say—the first twenty thousand words, but that after that one would be stuck. And all she did was say, "Well, I still think you ought to write about *real* things."

❧

Maybe she was right, though as I was seventy-nine when she gave me the advice I felt that this was not the right time to tell me.

The world of Bertie Wooster and his friends of the Drones Club, of which I have been writing since I was so high, is, I suppose, not only unreal but a thing of the past. It was always a small world—one of the smallest I ever met, as Bertie would say—and now it is not even small; it is nonexistent. It has gone with the wind and is one with Nineveh and Tyre.

This is pointed out to me every time a new book of mine dealing with the members of the Drones is published. "Edwardian!" the critics hiss at me. (It is not easy to hiss the word Edwardian, containing as it does no sibilant, but they manage it.) And I shuffle my feet and blush a good deal and say, "Yes, I suppose you're right, dash it." After all, I tell myself, there has been no generic name for the type of young man who figures in my stories since he used to be called a knut (or Gilbert the Filbert) in the pre-first-war days, which certainly seems to suggest that the species has died out like the macaronis of the Regency and the whiskered mashers of the Victoran era.

But sometimes I am in more defiant mood. Mine, I protest, are historical novels. Nobody objects when an author writes the sort of things that begin, "More skilled though I am at wielding the broadsword than the pen, I will set down for all to read the tale of how I, plain John Blunt, did follow my dear liege to the wars when Harry, yclept the fifth, sat on our English throne." So why am I not to be allowed to set down for all to read the tale of how the Hon. J. Blunt got fined five pounds by the magistrate at Bosher Street Police Court for disorderly conduct on Boat Race Night? Unfair discrimination is the phrase that springs to the lips.

No doubt one thing that makes these drones of mine seem creatures from a dead past is that with the exception of Oofy Prosser, the club millionaire, they are genial and good-tempered. In these days when everybody hates the insides of everybody else, anyone who is not snarling at something—or at everything—is an anachronism. The Edwardian knut was never an angry young man. He would get a little cross, perhaps, if his man Meadowes sent him out some morning with odd spats on, but his normal outlook on life was sunny. He was a humble, kindly soul who knew he was a silly ass but hoped you wouldn't mind. He liked everybody, and most people liked him. Portrayed on the stage by George Grossmith and G. P. Huntley, he was a lovable figure, warming the hearts of all. You might disapprove of him not being a world's worker, but you could not help being fond of him.

Though, as a matter of fact, many of the members of the Drones Club are world's workers. Freddie Threepwood, Lord Emsworth's younger son, is a vice-president at Donaldson's Dog Joy, Inc., of Long Island City and sells as smart a dog biscuit as the best of them. Bingo Little edits *Wee Tots*, the journal which has done so much to mold thought in the nursery. Catsmeat Potter-Pirbright has played the juvenile in a number of West End comedies, generally coming on early in Act One with a racket and a cheery "Tennis, anyone?" And even Bertie Wooster once wrote a thoughtful piece on What the Well-Dressed Man Is Wearing for his Aunt Dahlia's weekly, *Milady's Boudoir*. Your knut could always work if he felt like it. It was very seldom, of course, that he did feel like it. He preferred just to exist beautifully.

Two things caused the decline of the knut, the first of which was that hard times hit younger sons. Most knuts were younger sons, and in the reign of good King Edward the position of the younger son in aristocratic families was . . . what's the word, Jeeves? Anomalous? You're sure? Right ho, anomalous. Thank you, Jeeves. Putting it another way, he was a trifle on the superfluous side, his standing about that of the litter of kittens which the household cat deposits in the drawer where you keep your clean shirts.

What generally happened was this. An Earl, let us say, begat an heir. So far, so good. One can always do with an heir. But then— these Earls never know where to stop—he absentmindedly, as it were, begat a second son and this time was not any too pleased about the state of affairs. Unlike the male codfish which, becoming the father of 3,500,000 little codfish, cheerfully resolves to love them all, the aristocrat of those days found the younger son definitely a nuisance. Unless he went into the Church—which, as a rule, he stoutly declined to do—it was difficult to see how to fit him in. But there he was, requiring his calories just the same as if he had been the first in succession. It made the Earl feel that he was up against something hard to handle.

"Can't let Algy starve," he said to himself, and forked out a monthly allowance. And so there came into being a group of ornamental young men whom the ravens fed. Like the lilies of the field, they toiled not neither did they spin but lived quite contentedly on the paternal dole. Their wants were few. Provided they could secure the services of a tailor who was prepared to accept charm of manner as a substitute for ready cash—and it was extraordinary how full London was of altruistic tailors in the early 1900s—they asked for little more. In short, so long as the ravens continued to do their stuff, they were in that enviable condition known as sitting pretty.

Then the economic factor reared its ugly head. There were global wars, and if you have global wars, you cannot have happy, well-fed younger sons. Income tax and supertax shot up like those things they let off at Cape Canaveral, and the Earl found himself doing some constructive thinking. A bright idea occurred to him, and the more he turned it over in his mind, the better he liked it.

"*Why* can't I?" he said to his Countess as they sat one night trying to balance the budget.

"Why can't you what?" said the Countess.

"Let Algy starve?"

"Algy who?"

"Our Algy."

"You mean our second son, the Hon. Algernon Blair Tregennis Worthington ffinch-ffinch?"

"That's right. He's getting into my ribs to the tune of a cool thousand a year because I felt I couldn't let him starve. The point I'm making is why *not* let him starve?"

"It's a thought," the Countess agreed. "Yes, I think you've got something there. Probably do the young bounder good. We all eat too much these days, anyway."

So the ravens were retired from active duty, and Algy, faced with the prospect of not getting his three square meals a day unless he worked for them, hurried out and found a job, with the result that now any poor hack like myself who, wishing to turn an honest penny, writes stories about him and all the other Algys, Freddies, Bingos, Pongos, and Berties automatically finds himself labeled Edwardian.

The second thing that led to the elimination of the knut was the passing of the spat. In the brave old days spats were the hallmark of the young man about town, the foundation stone on which his whole policy was based, and it is sad to reflect that a generation has arisen which does not know what spats were. I once wrote a book called *Young Men in Spats*. I could not use that title today.

Spatterdashes was, I believe, their full name, and they were made of white cloth and buttoned around the ankles, partly no doubt to protect the socks from getting dashed with spatter but principally because they lent a sort of gay diablerie to the wearer's appearance. The monocle might or might not be worn, according to taste, but spats, like the tightly-rolled umbrella, were obligatory. I was never myself by knut standards really dressy as a young man (circa 1905), for a certain anemia of the exchequer compelled me to go about my social duties in my brother's cast-off frock coat and trousers, neither of which fitted me, and a top hat bequeathed to me by an uncle with a head some sizes larger than mine, but my umbrella was always rolled as tight as a drum, and though spats cost money, I had mine all right.

There they were, white and gleaming, fascinating the passerby and causing seedy strangers who hoped to share the wealth to address me as "Captain" and sometimes even as "M'lord." Many a butler at the turn of the century, opening the front door to me and wincing visibly at the sight of my topper, would lower his eyes, see the spats, and give a little sigh of relief, as much as to say, "Not quite what we are accustomed to at the northern end, perhaps, but unexceptionable to the south."

Naturally if you cut off a fellow's allowance, he cannot afford spats, and without spats he is a spent force. Deprived of these "musts," the knut threw in the towel and called it a day.

But I have not altogether lost hope of a revival of knuttery. The Drones, I feel, though crushed to earth, will rise again. With all the money people are paying to roam over the stately homes of England, those who own these homes will soon be in the chips again. (Am I wrong, or did I read in the paper that the Duke of Bedford had cleaned up £150,000 last year at Woburn Abbey? Well, even if it was only £50,000, that is unquestionably nice sugar and should ease the strain a lot.) Family fortunes will be restored, and if they are, there seems no reason to suppose that the younger son will not get his cut. I feel sure that, once the fountain of gold starts playing again, we shall have the knut with us once more.

At the moment, of course, every member of the Drones Club—and, for the matter of that, of Buck's and White's and Bellamy's—is an earnest young man immersed in some serious job who would raise his eyebrows coldly if you suggested that he steal a policeman's helmet on Boat Race Night, but I cannot believe that this austere attitude will be permanent. The heart of Young England is sound. Give the knut back his allowance, dangle a pair of spats before his eyes, and all the old fires will be renewed.

Already one sees signs of a coming renaissance. My spies inform me that the butler is creeping back. Extinct, it seemed, only a few years ago, he is now repeatedly seen again in his old haunts like some shy bird which, driven from its native marshes by alarms and excursions, stiffens the sinews, summons up the blood, and decides to give the old home another try. Who can say that ere long spats and knuts and all the old bung-ho-ing will not be flourishing again?

When that happens, I shall look my critics in the eye and say, "Edwardian, am I? Where do you get that Edwardian stuff? I write of life as it is lived today."

P.G.W.

1000 Park Avenue
New York
January 3, 1961

Dear Bill,

The letters arrived yesterday, and I have just finished a first quick perusal.

It gives one an odd feeling reading letters one has written over a period of forty years. Rather like drowning and having one's whole past life flash before one. How few of the people I mention are still alive. Guy Bolton, thank goodness, and Malcolm Muggeridge and Ira Gershwin and Frank Sullivan, also thank goodness, but Flo Ziegfeld, Charlie Dillingham, Ray Comstock, Marilyn Miller, Gertie Lawrence, Jerry Kern, George Gershwin, Lorimer, Wells, Kipling, Molnár . . . dozens of them, all gone, and you and I in a few months will be eighty.

Solemn thought, that. Makes one revise one's views. I had always supposed that the whole idea of the thing was that others might make the Obituary column but that I was immortal and would go on forever. I see now that I was mistaken, and that I, too, must ere long hand in my dinner pail. I'm not sure I like the new arrangement, but there it is.

It does seem silly that blokes as young and sprightly as you and me should have reached such an age as eighty. However, it has to be faced. I'm slowing up. I still do my before-breakfast exercises every morning, plus touching my toes fifty times without a suspicion of bending the knees, and I can navigate my daily three miles, but I can see I'm not quite the man I was.

Little things tell the story. When on my infrequent visits to New York a taxi driver nearly runs me down, he no longer damns my eyes and wants to know where I think I'm going; he shakes his head indulgently and says, "Watch it, grandpa!" Furthermore, I am noticeably less nimble when getting after the dog next door if I see him with his head and shoulders in our garbage can. And I note a certain stiffness of the limbs which causes me, when rising from my chair, to remind the beholder, if a man who has traveled in Equatorial Africa, of a hippopotamus heaving itself up from the mud of a riverbank.

Nevertheless, once one has got the knack of it, one comes to enjoy being what Somerset Maugham calls a "very old party." Life becomes more tranquil. The hot blood of the late seventies has cooled. Today when I see a sexagenarian—Frank Sullivan, as it might be, or somebody like that—climbing a tree, I smile and say to myself, "Boys will be boys. When you are my age, child," I say to myself, "you will realize that the true pleasures are mental." I am eighty and may quite easily go to par, and I find I am quite happy just sitting and thinking, or at any rate sitting. I can detach myself from the world. And if there is a better world to detach oneself from than the one functioning as of even date, I have yet to hear of it.

The great thing about being an octogenarian is that you can legitimately become set in your ways. I have always wanted to do this, but in the old days something was always happening to prevent it. There was never a chance of simply doing the same thing every day and being able to work regular hours without interruption, as I can now. One was perpetually dashing about, leaping from continent to continent, seeing editors, lunching with managers, going on the road with shows, popping off to Hollywood, popping back again, and generally behaving more like the jack-rabbit of the prairies than anything human. Today in my quiet rural retreat I do the same things day after day, with no variation. Morning exercises, breakfast, work till noon, watch *Love of Life* on television, lunch, take the dogs to the post office, walk back, more work, cocktails, dinner, and then the quiet evening with a Rex Stout or an Erle Stanley Gardner. Monotonous? Not a bit of it. I love it. The cry goes around Remsenburg, "Wodehouse has found his niche." And an octogenarian, mind you, is not expected to go to parties. The thought that I shall never have to wear a paper hat again is a very sustaining one.

There is, of course, the possibility of getting too set in one's ways. One recalls the case of the old gentleman of regular habits in the English country town who was accustomed to go every morning to the stationer's shop and buy his daily paper. At first the stationer would offer a word on the weather, but it was always received in silence. The old gentleman liked to walk in, pick up his paper, and walk out again without speaking.

This went on for fifteen years, and then the stationer moved to a larger shop on the other side of the street and his old establishment was taken over by a confectioner. Knowing his client's prejudice in favor of silence, the stationer made no mention to him of the impending change, and on the morning after it had taken place the creature of habit left his house as usual, turned in at the confectioner's to buy his paper, and dropped lifeless on the floor. The medical verdict was that when, pottering in, he saw a tray of French pastries where for fifteen years he had been seeing national newspapers, their sudden impact was too much for him and his heart ran into his liver or something of that sort.

This man was an extremist, and there is no need to carry the thing as far as he did, but basically he had the right idea.

Another compensation for being a very old party is that by the time you reach eighty you have become more tolerant. Your kid of seventy-five is full of juvenile prejudices, but we octogenarians are able to take the broader, kindlier view. We accept someone like Fidel Castro or Nikita Khrushchev as part of the great plan, knowing that he must have been put into the world for some purpose, though with our finite minds we cannot understand what that purpose was. Perhaps we are not meant to understand.

So, on the whole, I have no objection to being 80. Fortunately, perhaps, for there seems to be nothing I can do about it.